The Essential Jewish Cookbook

the
Essential Jewish Cookbook

100 Easy Recipes for the Modern Jewish Kitchen

MARCIA FRIEDMAN

ROCKRIDGE
PRESS

For Daryl.
For our parents, Sandra, Berney, Gloria, and David. And for
everyone seeking an entrée to the wonderful world of Jewish food.

For general information on our other products and services or to obtain technical support, please contact our Customer Care Department within the United States at (866) 744-2665, or outside the United States at (510) 253-0500.

Rockridge Press publishes its books in a variety of electronic and print formats. Some content that appears in print may not be available in electronic books, and vice versa.

TRADEMARKS: Rockridge Press and the Rockridge Press logo are trademarks or registered trademarks of Callisto Media Inc. and/or its affiliates, in the United States and other countries, and may not be used without written permission. All other trademarks are the property of their respective owners. Rockridge Press is not associated with any product or vendor mentioned in this book.

Interior and Cover Designer: Richard Tapp
Art Producer: Hannah Dickerson
Editor: Claire Yee
Production Editor: Rachel Taenzler

Photography © 2020 Hélène Dujardin, food styling by Anna Hampton, cover; © Hélène Dujardin, p. 94; Mariela Naplatanova/Stocksy, p. VI; vladi79/iStock.com, p. VIII; Emily Clifton/StockFood, p. 14; Leigh Beisch/StockFood, p. 34; Sean Locke/Stocksy, p. 52; Nadine Greeff/Stocksy, p. 76; Harald Walker/Stocksy, p. 118; The Picture Pantry/StockFood, p. 136; Noemi Hauser/Stocksy, p. 154; Sarka Babicka/StockFood, p. 178. Decorative pattern © Curly Pat/Creative Market. Author photo courtesy of Marcia Friedman.

ISBN: Print 978-1-64611-727-7
eBook 978-1-64611-728-4
R1

Contents

Introduction

After converting to Judaism more than two decades ago, my first stop (after the synagogue) was the kitchen. Without a Jewish upbringing, I found the best way I could explore the rich history of my new culture was through food. However, there was little in the way of a one-stop shop for easy, essential Jewish recipes.

I was looking for a book like this one and couldn't find it. So, now I've written it. This book is for me and for you: the home cook looking for a cookbook steeped in tradition, but relevant to today's modern tastes. The friendly, approachable recipes include vegetarian, gluten-free, and kosher options and—since Jewish foods have a place at every American table—are accessible to everyone, no matter your religion.

Since food, culture, and history are inseparable, we'll also explore the historical context of the recipes. Use this book as your tour guide for a culinary journey through Jewish history, from the Middle East to Europe, from North Africa to the Americas, and beyond.

I've savored exploring Jewish food, history, and culture, and I'm happy to be able to share all I've learned with you. I hope this book is the written equivalent of chicken soup—a "cure-all" for anytime you need the warm, healing power of Jewish food.

Chapter 1

A Rich Nibble of History

Jewish culinary tradition is sometimes described as a tapestry, and aptly so. Over thousands of years, the threads of Jewish culture and cuisine have interwoven with food cultures from all around the world, fostering a unique way of cooking and eating. Before we start cooking, let's explore the forces and history that led us to the vibrant Jewish cooking we know today.

A Celebration of Culinary Tradition

Jewish culinary tradition thrived over thousands of years and thousands of miles. Many forces shaped it, but two made an indelible impact.

First: rules. Historically, Jewish dietary practices and the observance of Shabbat (the Jewish day of rest) influenced what and how Jews ate. Kosher rules governed permissible foods and preparations, resulting in uniquely Jewish cooking and recipes. The prohibition of cooking on Shabbat resulted in a long tradition of slow-cooked stews, delicious cold salads, and other make-ahead foods.

Second: movement. The creation of the Jewish diaspora after 70 CE forced Jews from their ancient homeland in biblical Israel, scattering them into new or existing Jewish communities worldwide. Faced with repeated religious persecution, they would move again and again, making displacement a major feature of Jewish history. As Jews moved, they adapted local culinary customs, recipes, and ingredients for Shabbat and other holiday observances (as well as kosher law). When displaced again, they would carry these on to the next home, spreading food traditions to new places.

Out of this comes the dynamic and global Jewish cuisine of today, including everything from bagels to baba ghanoush and beyond. In discussing Jewish cuisine, we often identify it by Ashkenazi, Sephardi, and Mizrahi traditions. These aren't all-inclusive categories, but they help us begin to explore Jewish history and culinary evolution.

Ashkenazi—of Bubbes and Bagels

If bagels, latkes, matzah ball soup, brisket, and challah are on your list of the most iconic Jewish foods, you are not alone. These foods, often lovingly associated with Yiddish-speaking Jewish *bubbes* (grandmas), originated from the kitchens of Ashkenazi Jews, part of the diaspora that settled in Germany and France and spread to Eastern Europe. As they moved around the world, they carried with them their foodways. Ashkenazi Jews make up the majority of Jews in the United States today, so it's no surprise that their cuisine made a big impact on American cuisine, among Jews and non-Jews alike.

Traditions

Ashkenazi Jewish culinary traditions center on a handful of core elements, including:

* breads, such as challah, rye bread, babka, bagels, and the bialy—a round, bagel-like bread with a flattened center filled with diced onions
* pickled foods, such as pickles, sauerkraut, pickled herring, and cured and smoked meats that could be stored for long periods of time; and strong-flavored ingredients such as onions, garlic, and dill
* root vegetables, especially potatoes, carrots, and beets
* stuffed foods, such as blintzes, knishes, kreplach, stuffed cabbage, and pierogis, often eaten on holidays (traditional gefilte fish also was originally stuffed)
* sweets, including cheesecakes, macaroons, mandelbrot, rugelach, hamantaschen, and sweets using fruit, like apple cake
* warm comfort foods, including stewed meats like brisket and slow-cooked stews (cholent) as well as chicken soup (sometimes called "Jewish penicillin"), served with egg noodles or matzah balls

Origins

The Ashkenazi Jewish story began in medieval times, when part of the Jewish diaspora settled in *shtetls* (villages) in what is now modern-day Germany and France ("Ashkenaz" is a medieval rabbinical name for Germany). Out of this early European life emerged the Yiddish language, derived from German dialects and peppered with Hebrew and other languages. Of course, many distinct foods emerged as well.

Ashkenazi cuisine was strongly influenced by geography. Cold European winters meant relying on hardy root vegetables and cured foods that stored well. Jewish cooks also embraced existing local favorites, such as French chopped liver and German braided breads, which became challah. They incorporated foods introduced by Jewish traders, such as noodles from Italy. And, of course, they adapted local dishes to make them kosher and for Shabbat and holiday observances (such as replacing bread dumplings with matzah balls for Passover).

In the late Middle Ages, religious persecution forced Ashkenazi Jews east, mainly to Poland and Russia. They took German-influenced traditions with them and adopted new Eastern European dishes, like bagels, blintzes, and borscht. In the late nineteenth century, poverty and persecution spurred yet another mass migration of Ashkenazi Jews, especially to North America.

Evolution

By 1924, two million Eastern European Jews had immigrated to the United States, establishing enclaves in places like Boston, Philadelphia, and most notably, New York City's Lower East Side. World War II and the tragedy of the Holocaust, when six million Jews were killed in Europe, further spurred Ashkenazi Jewish migration to the United States (and also Israel, Latin America, South Africa, and Australia). As Jews sought to reestablish themselves stateside, their foods both influenced and were influenced by American culture.

Early on, Jewish delicatessens sprang up to sell kosher pickled, cured, and smoked items and eventually full meals. Popular delis introduced Jewish foods like pastrami and corned beef to non-Jewish populations. Older, more labor-intensive foods, like *kishke* (stuffed intestines) and homemade gefilte fish (which often involved temporarily keeping a live carp in your bathtub—yes, really) gradually fell out of favor with the advent of time-saving appliances and canned and frozen foods.

Jews adapted their Eastern European foodways with new ingredients to great effect. Take cream cheese, invented in New York in the 1870s. In the early twentieth century, Jews adopted cream cheese to "schmear" (spread) on bagels, and Jewish bakers substituted cream cheese for curd cheese in baking, paving the way for New York–style cheesecake. Modern Jewish cooks continue to use new ingredients to tinker with traditional foods, such as gefilte fish made with salmon or latkes made with sweet potatoes. Even after centuries of experimentation, though, beloved Ashkenazic classics live on, preserving ties to Jewish tradition and community.

Sephardi—Mediterranean Melding

Sephardi Jews were among the first to immigrate to America, arriving as early as 1654—but Sephardi culinary traditions are less well known historically in the United States. Sephardi Judaism originated in what is now modern-day Spain and Portugal. ("Sepharad" refers to the Iberian Peninsula.) These Jews lived there for centuries—where they developed a Judeo-Spanish hybrid language, Ladino—until their expulsion by Spain's Catholic monarchs in 1492.

Sephardi Jews spread across several regions all around the Mediterranean as well as Northern Europe, the Americas, and beyond, and their movement to the Middle East and North Africa created an even more fascinating melding of traditions.

Traditions

Sephardi food varies greatly, but think of it as Jewish Mediterranean food with significant Spanish and Middle Eastern influences. Sephardi Jewish cooking emphasizes foods found in the temperate Mediterranean climate, including fruits, vegetables, herbs, nuts, and olive oil.

For Shabbat, traditions include slow-cooked stews (hamin) prepared before sundown and cooked vegetable salads and sweet-and-sour dishes that can be served at room temperature or cold. On Hanukkah, when Jews eat oil-fried foods, Sephardi Jews might serve fried chicken and deep-fried fritters, such as bimuelos (also called buñuelos). Some hallmarks of Sephardi cuisine include:

* chickpeas and lentils
* custards and puddings
* dishes with eggs
* eggplant
* handheld pastries, such as bourekas
* meat-and-fruit combinations, such as chicken with apricots or apples
* nuts, especially almonds and pine nuts
* olive oil for cooking
* onions and garlic
* orange blossom water and rose water
* rice
* sweet-and-sour flavors, in everything from braised peppers to meatballs
* tomato-based sauces and stews

Origins

The Sephardi story began thousands of years ago, when Jews established communities in Spain, even before the destruction of the Second Temple in Jerusalem in 70 CE. When Spain came under Muslim rule from roughly the seventh to thirteenth centuries, the Jews (and other non-Muslims) there enjoyed a relatively peaceful and civilized period.

Muslim rulers introduced culinary practices that Jews adopted, such as double-cooking, as well as new ingredients, including raisins and pine nuts. To keep kosher, Jewish cooks used olive oil instead of the pork fat used by their neighbors and the butter preferred by Arab cooks. They also embraced foods introduced by traders, including eggplant, which is featured in many Jewish recipes, and produce brought back by Spanish colonizers of the New World, such as onions and tomatoes.

In Italy, a separate Jewish community mostly flourished for much of the same period through World War II. Italian Jews are sometimes grouped under the Sephardi umbrella due to proximity and the influence of Sephardi refugees from Spain, but they existed as a separate community that spoke Italian and had their own richly varied Jewish-Italian cuisine (which I cover in my book, *Meatballs and Matzah Balls*).

Evolution

Christian conquerors reclaimed Spain from Muslim rule in the thirteenth century. Gradually resentment and violence toward Jews grew. Under pressure, some Jews converted to Christianity. "Conversos," as they were called, sometimes continued their Jewish culinary customs, like avoiding pork and observing Shabbat—practices that could mark them for arrest and persecution if discovered by the Spanish Inquisition, which sought to eliminate nonadherents to Christianity.

In 1492, the Alhambra Decree ordered practicing Jews be expelled from Spain. This huge event scattered Sephardi Jewish communities—and their traditions—far and wide, including the Americas and Northern Europe (where incidentally Portuguese exiles introduced their recipe for batter-fried fish, later widely adopted as fish and chips). A large number of Sephardi Jews headed eastward, resettling in regions across the Mediterranean and the vast holdings of the Ottoman Empire in southeastern Europe, North Africa, and the Middle East, including what would become British-controlled Palestine. As they joined existing Mizrahi Jewish communities, especially in places like Morocco, they notably melded their traditions with local cuisine.

Following the end of British rule and the passage of the UN partition plan, Israel declared independence in 1948. With the reestablishment of a Jewish state in ancient Israel, Jews in Muslim-majority countries faced increased hostility. Many relocated to Israel or the United States, carrying their rich food traditions on to a new chapter.

Mizrahi—Embracing the "East"

For many years, all non-Ashkenazi Jews were referred to as Sephardi. But that binary failed to capture the experience of many Jews who lived in a wide region stretching from Greece to North Africa for thousands of years before Sephardi migration. In recent decades, the term "Mizrahi" (meaning "east" in Hebrew) has come into use to refer to Jews who lived continuously in areas around the Middle East but are not of Iberian descent.

When we think of Mizrahi food, hummus, falafel, skewered grilled meats, and rice may spring to mind. The reality is more complex, though—the foodways of Mizrahi Jews over thousands of years represent a diverse cross-section of regions, histories, and cultures.

Traditions

Mizrahi food traditions encompass a wide range of Mediterranean, North African, Arab, Indian, and Persian culinary customs. They also sometimes reflect the influence of Sephardi Jews who settled in the region after 1492. Many Mizrahi food traditions have strong roots in specific regions, resulting in Jewish versions of dishes like moussaka from Greece and biryani from the Indian subcontinent. In places where Jewish communities were more isolated, distinct dishes emerged, such as malawach, a flaky flatbread developed by Yemenite Jews.

Some common features of this wide-ranging tradition include:
* aromatic spice blends, sauces, and pastes, such as zhug
* chickpea preparations, including stews, hummus, and falafel
* colorful chopped salads
* cooked vegetable salads
* flatbreads, such as pita, malawach, laffa, and lavash
* ground meats and meat-stuffed dumplings
* meat and rice dishes incorporating dried fruits
* olive oil for cooking
* orange blossom water and rose water
* rice and couscous as staples, as well as in special dishes such as Moroccan seven-vegetable couscous served for Rosh Hashanah
* skewered and grilled meats
* slow-cooked stews, such as Ethiopian doro wot
* stuffed vegetables

* tomato-based stews, such as shakshuka
* turnovers, such as sambousak and bourekas

Origins

Mizrahi Jewish history takes us all the way back to the early sixth century BCE, when the Babylonian siege of Jerusalem led to the exile of roughly 10,000 Jews from Jerusalem to Babylon (modern-day Iraq). Some Jews were able to return to Jerusalem, but many stayed in Babylon, which became a bastion of Jewish learning, progress, life, and culture in the diaspora until the eleventh century.

Over time, Jews of the Babylonian exile settled in several regions, where they developed and maintained close cultural ties to their local communities. Unlike Ashkenazi and Sephardi Jews, Mizrahi Jews often spoke local languages (predominantly Arabic or Farsi), rather than a separate language like Yiddish or Ladino.

Because home regions remain central to Mizrahi Jewish identity, it's helpful to understand the places they have populated: North Africa (including modern-day Algeria, Egypt, Morocco, Tunisia, and Yemen); the Middle East (including modern-day Iran, Iraq, Israel, Lebanon, and Syria); Western/Central Asia, Southeastern Europe, and the Eastern Mediterranean (including modern-day Afghanistan, Armenia, Cyprus, Georgia, Greece, Turkey, and Uzbekistan, around the city of Bukhara); and India. Ethiopian Jews are sometimes grouped in with Mizrahi Jews, but they are their own separate ancient community with distinct religious observances.

Evolution

The Spanish expulsion of Jews in 1492 led to an influx of Sephardi immigrants into Mizrahi communities. In regions where Sephardim arrived in large numbers, like Morocco, the cuisines melded. Mizrahi dishes like adafina and the sweet pancakes called mufleta, eaten for Mimouna (the Mizrahi Jewish celebration marking the end of Passover), reflect a Spanish influence.

After Israel declared independence in 1948, hostility toward Jews from surrounding Muslim-led countries prompted many Mizrahi Jews—both by choice and by force—to immigrate to Israel and the United States. In subsequent decades, coordinated Israeli and American efforts fostered Jewish emigration and helped evacuate Jews under duress (such as from Ethiopia and Yemen) to Israel in great numbers. As a result, very few Mizrahi Jews remain in their countries of origin today.

Mizrahi traditions have been welcomed and celebrated in Israel and beyond. The Ethiopian Jewish fall holiday *Sigd*, a half-day of fasting and prayers followed by a festival meal of traditional Ethiopian food, became an official holiday in Israel in 2008. Foods from Mizrahi traditions, such as Lebanese tabbouleh and Turkish bourekas, have been warmly adopted, especially in Israel and also the United States. Celebrations such as Mimouna have caught on as well.

Today

This arc of history and experience has produced a remarkable and uniquely global food culture. It is one rooted in traditions, experiences, adaptation, perseverance, and celebration, as well as influenced by the many places Jews have called home. It remains dynamic and delicious.

It wouldn't be unusual for today's home tables to display a vibrant cross section of Jewish culinary traditions. For instance, think of a Rosh Hashanah dinner of Turkish and Egyptian black-eyed peas, Moroccan couscous, Sephardi and Jewish-Italian sautéed spinach with pine nuts, and Ashkenazi brisket and tzimmes, with honey-soaked Middle Eastern baklava for dessert.

Meanwhile, restaurant owners, food writers, and home cooks are experimenting with traditional dishes and cooking methods (such as smoking and curing) and reinventing them with regional flair and modern, personal touches. The celebratory fusion of foods and traditions shows no sign of stopping, and examples—from za'atar challah to food historian Michael W. Twitty's West African brisket—continue to delight everyone.

So go ahead and pull some threads on this intricate tapestry and follow a trail of culinary wonder. It connects Jews everywhere to thousands of years of history and survival—and to each other.

KEEPING KOSHER

Jewish dietary laws, which are called kashrut, have shaped Jewish cooking and recipes for thousands of years. Although kosher observance varies widely today among many modern and secular Jews, most classically Jewish recipes are kosher. Accordingly, most of the recipes in this book generally align with kosher rules, either as written or through included variations.

Here's a quick overview of kosher law. It prohibits consumption of:

* certain animals (such as shellfish, reptiles, insects, some birds, and any mammal without cloven hooves and that doesn't chew its cud, such as pigs) and certain parts of permitted animals
* blood (it must be drained or broiled out of any meat to be eaten)
* dairy and meat foods prepared together or eaten at the same meal (foods like eggs, nuts, fruits, and vegetables are considered neutral [pareve] and can be eaten with either meat or dairy)
* meat not slaughtered according to Jewish law

In the Kitchen

Having certain tools and ingredients on hand can make the recipes easier and more enjoyable to create. Read on to find my recommended list of equipment and ingredients, as well as some frequently used techniques.

Equipment

I recommend: good sharp knives (particularly a chef's knife, serrated or bread knife, and paring knife), a blender or an immersion blender, a small food processor, a handheld mixer, a Dutch oven or deep heavy pot, a deep-fry thermometer, and an instant-read thermometer. A large food processor and stand mixer come in handy, but are not necessary.

Also note that success will often rely on monitoring the cooking carefully. Cooktops, ovens, and cookware heat differently, so check on your food well before the timer goes off, and adjust settings and cook times as needed. If your baked goods are browning too quickly, cover them loosely with foil to prevent burning.

Ingredients

Chicken or vegetable stock. Store-bought stocks speed up cooking in many dishes, from braises and stews to rice and grains. Homemade stocks will boost flavor—use them whenever possible.

Eggs. Sephardi recipes frequently feature eggs, but so do Ashkenazi kugels and Passover dishes. Use large eggs, unless otherwise noted.

Matzah. This unleavened bread, central to Passover, is eaten across traditions. It's featured in several recipes, such as Matzah Brei with Lox and Dill (page 24). Matzah meal (ground up matzah) is used to make matzah balls and can be used in latkes or as a substitute for breadcrumbs.

Nuts (especially walnuts, pecans, almonds, pistachios, and pine nuts). Nuts are used in haroset for Passover as well as in sweets such as Mandelbrot (page 157). They're also a frequent garnish.

Oil. Mediterranean Jewish cuisines use olive oil as a main cooking fat and dressing, as do most of my recipes. For recipes for fried foods, keep plenty of vegetable oil on hand.

Onions and garlic. These ingredients figure prominently in recipes across Jewish cooking traditions.

Salt. These recipes were developed using Morton kosher salt. To substitute, for 1 teaspoon of Morton kosher salt, use about ¾ teaspoon fine table salt or about 1¾ teaspoons Diamond Crystal kosher salt. When in doubt, start with less and add more to taste.

Techniques

Braising. Slow-cooking dishes over low heat (in a covered pot with liquid) was and is an especially important technique. It is used to cook stews overnight on Shabbat and helps break down tough cuts of meat, like brisket. A Dutch oven or other deep-sided pan, as well as a roasting pan, are excellent for braised dishes.

Frying. Many favorite Jewish foods are fried—cooked in oil over high heat—like potato latkes, batter-fried fish, fried chicken, falafel, and donuts. Use enough vegetable oil to partially or fully submerge foods. For latkes, use a heavy-bottomed pan, like a cast-iron skillet. For deep-frying, use a deeper pot, like a Dutch oven. A deep-fry or candy thermometer is helpful to keep the oil temperature in a proper and safe range.

Making Ahead. In Jewish tradition, cooking is prohibited on Shabbat—the day of rest. As such, many traditional dishes are meant to be made ahead and enjoyed cold or at room temperature.

Stuffing. Jewish tradition includes many stuffed or filled foods, from cabbage and grape leaves to peppers and squash, to cookies and dried fruit. Stuffed foods often symbolize abundance and are popular on holidays, especially Sukkot.

About the Recipes

Choosing 100 recipes from thousands of years of culinary history was not an undertaking I took lightly. During my search for the most beloved and storied recipes across Ashkenazi, Sephardi, and Mizrahi traditions, I reviewed a vast array of Jewish cookbooks, articles, and other resources. My recipes here are a combination of well-known dishes, foods symbolic for holidays, everyday favorites, and foods that help tell parts of the Jewish story. The headnotes share a little of each recipe's historical context.

To me, a recipe is "essential" when it is a thread in the larger tapestry of Jewish culture and cuisine. Essential recipes should also be accessible and appealing to modern cooks interested in Jewish food. There is so much I couldn't include for lack of space, but think of these recipes as your starter set—good introductions to classic dishes at their very best.

I hope these recipes become reliable old friends that find their way to your kitchen again and again. Most recipes have manageable ingredient lists and straightforward preparations. Some recipes worth including require more steps to be their best—but don't worry, I walk you through them. Also, the recipes often include tips and shortcuts as well as labels (such as family-friendly, gluten-free, kosher, and vegetarian), so that you can make them to fit your own preferences and tastes.

When I converted to Judaism, one aspect of Jewish life that caught my attention early on was the love of questioning, from the great Talmudic arguments to modern-day disagreements about the best consistency of a matzah ball. What I've counted as essential and what you count as essential might not exactly match, but I hope you find this collection a thought-provoking starting place for creating your own treasury of Jewish favorite recipes.

Cheese Blintzes with Blueberry Sauce
Page 18

Chapter 2

Breakfast & Brunch

THE JEWISH DELI: FROM PUSHCART TO CULINARY INSTITUTION

Waves of Jewish immigrants from Germany and Eastern Europe arrived in America from the mid-1800s through the early twentieth century, especially in New York City—and they needed to eat. Jewish entrepreneurs began selling groceries and prepared foods from pushcarts and small stores, including old-country comforts like cured and pickled meats and fish and dill pickles. The Jewish delicatessen, a uniquely American institution, was born—and the rest is culinary history.

The delicatessens and their sister stores that sold dairy goods (called "appetizing shops" in New York City) became social hubs and also emblems of Jewish culture and cuisine. Over time, many became non-kosher "Jewish-style" delis that sold meat and dairy products together. Several dishes with Ashkenazi roots became smash hits, like pastrami (a New York deli innovation) and corned beef sandwiches, cured and pickled fish, matzah ball soup, latkes, chopped liver, blintzes, knishes, rugelach, and cheesecake, and even the non-kosher Reuben, a thick sandwich of corned beef, sauerkraut, and Swiss cheese on rye.

In recent years, renewed interest in Jewish comfort foods has bolstered venerable institutions—such as Katz's Delicatessen and Russ & Daughters Café in New York City, and Canter's Deli and Langer's Delicatessen in LA—and has seeded a new crop of Jewish-style artisanal delis nationwide. These ever-evolving institutions are a treasury of what late food historian Gil Marks termed "American Jewish soul food."

Challah French Toast

FAMILY-FRIENDLY, KOSHER, VEGETARIAN / SERVES 4 TO 6
PREP TIME: 20 minutes / **COOK TIME:** 10 minutes

Rich and pillowy challah bread, when soaked in milk and eggs and then fried golden brown, makes a superlative French toast. Challah French toast is a staple of many deli cafés and home kitchens, and it's a great way to use bread left over after Shabbat.

---

1 egg

1 egg yolk

2 tablespoons unsalted butter, melted, plus more for frying

1 cup whole milk

2 teaspoons vanilla extract

⅓ cup all-purpose flour

2 tablespoons sugar

¼ teaspoon cinnamon

¼ teaspoon kosher salt

5 to 6 slices day-old Challah (page 140), about ¾-inch thick (or store-bought)

Confectioners' sugar or maple syrup, for serving (optional)

---

1. Heat a large heavy skillet over medium heat until very hot.

2. In a blender, combine the egg, egg yolk, 2 tablespoons of melted butter, milk, vanilla extract, flour, sugar, cinnamon, and salt. Process until smooth.

3. Pour the egg mixture into a shallow dish. Soak the challah in the mixture until saturated but not falling apart, 1 to 2 minutes per side.

4. Melt 1 to 2 tablespoons of butter in the hot skillet, swirling to coat. Cook battered slices until golden and crisp, turning once, 1 to 2 minutes per side. Repeat with remaining challah, adding butter as needed.

5. Serve hot with confectioners' sugar or maple syrup, if using.

Cheese Blintzes with Blueberry Sauce

KOSHER, VEGETARIAN / SERVES 6 TO 8 (MAKES 10 TO 11 BLINTZES)
PREP TIME: 10 minutes / **COOK TIME:** 25 minutes

Blintzes first appeared on Jewish tables when Ashkenazi Jews lived in Romania, Ukraine, and Poland, and they skyrocketed to popularity when Jewish immigrants brought them to the United States. Among the many versions, sweet cheese–filled are most popular—and are also traditional for holidays when dairy foods are savored, like Shavuot and Hanukkah. For a shortcut, use warmed fruit preserves instead of the blueberry sauce.

FOR THE BLUEBERRY SAUCE

¾ cup sugar, or more to taste

1½ tablespoons cornstarch

3 cups (1 12-ounce package) frozen unsweetened blueberries, not thawed

¾ cup water

2 tablespoons freshly squeezed orange juice, or more to taste

FOR THE BLINTZES

1 recipe for Blintz Pancakes (page 151) or 1 package store-bought crepes

2 cups whole milk ricotta cheese, drained

6 ounces cream cheese, room temperature

½ tablespoon cornstarch

¼ cup confectioners' sugar

½ teaspoon ground cinnamon

1 teaspoon vanilla extract

½ teaspoon kosher salt

2 tablespoons unsalted butter, for frying blintzes

Confectioners' sugar and sour cream, for serving

TO MAKE THE BLUEBERRY SAUCE

1. In a medium saucepan, combine the sugar and cornstarch. Stir in the blueberries to coat, and then stir in the water. Bring the mixture to a boil over medium heat, and stir constantly until the mixture thickens and the blueberries are soft, 5 to 10 minutes.

2. Remove from the heat, stir in the orange juice to taste and add more sugar, if needed. Serve warm or refrigerate and reheat when ready to use.

TO MAKE THE BLINTZES

3. Prepare blintz pancakes, if necessary.

4. In a medium bowl, combine the ricotta, cream cheese, cornstarch, sugar, cinnamon, vanilla extract, and salt until smooth.

5. Place one pancake browned-side up on a plate. Spoon a scant ¼ cup of filling across the lower third in a wide ribbon, leaving a 1-inch border on the sides and bottom. Fold the bottom edge over the filling, then fold in the sides and roll up to form a rectangle. Repeat with remaining pancakes. (An alternate method: Spoon the filling in the center, tuck two sides toward the center, and then fold the top and bottom like an envelope.)

6. In a large skillet over medium-low heat, melt 1 tablespoon of butter. When hot, add half the blintzes in a single layer, seam-side down. Fry until golden brown, turning once, 2 to 3 minutes per side. Repeat with remaining butter and blintzes.

7. Serve hot with confectioners' sugar, sour cream, and blueberry sauce (or warmed preserves).

MAKE AHEAD TIP: Freeze assembled blintzes for up to 1 month. Fry directly from the freezer, loosely covered and over low heat to ensure the filling warms through.

Potato and Caramelized Onion Knishes

KOSHER, VEGETARIAN / SERVES 6 TO 8
PREP TIME: 40 minutes, plus 30 minutes resting time / **COOK TIME:** 1 hour

Knishes—small savory or sweet filled pies—were popularized in the United States by Ashkenazi immigrants from Ukraine and Poland. A filling grab-and-go snack, knishes became a staple of delis and street carts. They remain a Jewish comfort food classic today, with fillings ranging from cheese to sweet potato to pizza. This is my recipe for the enduring favorite: the potato knish. The steps take some time but are worth it, and you can make the knishes ahead (see tip).

FOR THE DOUGH
½ cup warm water
½ cup extra-virgin olive oil
1 teaspoon kosher salt
1 teaspoon white vinegar
2¾ to 3 cups all-purpose flour, plus more as needed

FOR THE FILLING
Extra-virgin olive oil

1½ large sweet onions, cut in half through the root end and thinly sliced
Kosher salt
Freshly ground black pepper
2 medium russet potatoes (about 1½ pounds), peeled and cut into chunks

FOR BAKING
Egg wash (1 egg, lightly beaten with 1 tablespoon cold water)

TO MAKE THE DOUGH

1. In a large bowl, mix together the water, oil, salt, and vinegar. Slowly add in 2¾ cups of flour and stir to combine.

2. Knead the dough a few times in the bowl to form a smooth dough, adding additional flour as needed. Divide the dough into 2 balls, cover, and let rest for 30 minutes at room temperature.

TO MAKE THE FILLING

3. Warm a layer of extra-virgin olive oil in a large skillet over medium-low heat. Add the onion and season lightly with salt and pepper to taste. Toss to coat, cover, and cook for about 10 minutes until softened.

4. Reduce the heat to low, uncover, and cook 10 more minutes or until deep golden brown, stirring occasionally.

5. Meanwhile, put the potatoes in a large saucepan and add water to cover by 1 inch. Salt the water and bring to a boil. Simmer, partially covered, until tender, about 20 minutes. Drain and mash, seasoning with additional salt and pepper.

6. Combine the potatoes and onions. Set aside.

TO MAKE THE KNISHES

7. Preheat the oven to 400°F and line a large sheet pan with parchment paper.

8. Working with one dough ball at a time, on a lightly floured surface (or between two sheets of wax paper) roll the dough approximately ⅛ inch thick. Use a 2¾-inch biscuit cutter or drinking glass to cut into rounds.

9. Place a scant 1 tablespoon of filling in the center of each round. Fold up the sides, pinching to close. Reroll the dough scraps and repeat.

10. Place the knishes seam-side down on the sheet pan. Brush the tops with egg wash and bake until golden brown, 20 to 30 minutes. Serve warm or at room temperature.

MAKE AHEAD TIP: Freeze the baked and cooled knishes and reheat as needed. Bake at 375° F, loosely covered with foil, 15 to 20 minutes or until hot.

Shakshuka (Eggs Poached in Spicy Tomato Sauce)

GLUTEN-FREE, KOSHER, VEGETARIAN / SERVES 6
PREP TIME: 10 minutes / **COOK TIME:** 30 minutes

Shakshuka's origins are disputed, but it is common in North African cuisines and was likely brought to Israel by Tunisian Jews. Recipes vary, but this straightforward version is vibrant in color and flavor—don't forget some bread to mop up all the sauce and yolks.

Extra-virgin olive oil
1 small sweet onion, finely chopped
Kosher salt
Freshly ground black pepper
3 garlic cloves, minced
½ to 1 teaspoon crushed red pepper flakes

1 (14.5-ounce) can crushed tomatoes
1 (14.5-ounce) can diced tomatoes with juices
6 eggs
8 ounces ricotta, for serving (optional)

---

1. In large nonstick skillet over medium-high heat, warm a layer of olive oil. Add the onion and season with salt and pepper to taste. Cook, stirring frequently, until softened, 3 to 5 minutes. Add the garlic and red pepper flakes and cook for 1 minute, stirring constantly.

2. Add both cans of tomatoes and reduce the heat. Simmer until a thick sauce forms, about 15 minutes. Season to taste.

3. Make 6 wells in the sauce, and break an egg into each well. Sprinkle the eggs with black pepper and loosely cover the pan with foil or a lid. Cook until the eggs are cooked to preference, 5 to 10 minutes.

4. Remove from the heat, let rest several minutes, and serve with a dollop of ricotta (if using).

MAKE AHEAD TIP: Prepare the sauce ahead and keep refrigerated for up to 3 days.

Blueberry and Cream Cheese Bourekas

KOSHER, VEGETARIAN / SERVES 4 TO 6
PREP TIME: 20 minutes, plus 15 minutes thawing / **COOK TIME:** 15 minutes

Bourekas are a mouthwatering Sephardi melding of Spanish empanadas and Turkish borek that emerged from Jewish life in the Ottoman Empire. Today, these pastry turnovers are immensely popular in Israel in a range of doughs and fillings—especially savory fillings like potato, cheese, or spinach. Sweet fillings are less traditional but equally crowd-pleasing for brunch or dessert. Here's my deliciously easy blueberry-cheese version using store-bought puff pastry.

1 sheet frozen store-bought puff pastry
About ⅔ cup blueberry preserves

5 ounces cream cheese, divided
   into 9 pieces
Cooking spray

1. Thaw puff pastry according to package instructions (usually around 15 minutes).

2. Preheat the oven to 400°F and line a sheet pan with parchment paper.

3. On a lightly floured surface, roll the pastry into a 9-by-9-inch square. Cut into 9 squares and roll each square to about 5-by-5 inches.

4. Place 2½ heaping teaspoons of preserves in the middle of each square and top with 1 piece of cream cheese (slightly flattened).

5. Dampen the outer pastry edges with water and fold the dough over the filling to make a triangle. Pinch the ends firmly and crimp the edges with a fork.

6. Transfer the bourekas to the sheet pan, gently pierce the tops with a fork to allow steam to escape, and lightly coat with cooking spray.

7. Bake for 15 minutes, until puffy and golden. Cool slightly before serving.

Matzah Brei with Lox and Dill

FAMILY-FRIENDLY, KOSHER / SERVES 4
PREP TIME: 10 minutes / **COOK TIME:** 5 minutes

Matzah brei (pronounced like "fry") is softened matzah coated with eggs and then fried. The finished result falls somewhere between an omelet and a pancake. This Ashkenazi comfort food—prepared both sweet and savory—is a popular Passover breakfast. My savory version is garnished with two classics of Ashkenazi cuisine: lox and dill.

---

4 large sheets matzah, broken into 2- to 3-inch pieces

3 cups boiling water

4 eggs, lightly beaten

Freshly ground black pepper

Kosher salt

2 tablespoons unsalted butter

2 ounces lox or smoked salmon, sliced into 1-inch slivers, for garnish

1 tablespoon chopped fresh dill, for garnish

---

1. Place the matzah in a colander in the sink. Slowly pour the boiling water over the matzah to soften it, shaking the colander to drain.

2. In a large bowl, combine the matzah, eggs, and pepper to taste. Salt only lightly, since lox is salty. Let sit for 2 to 4 minutes, until the matzah is no longer crisp.

3. In a large nonstick skillet over medium-high heat, melt the butter. When foaming subsides, add the matzah mixture and cook, turning frequently, until the eggs are just set. Serve immediately, garnished with lox and dill.

VARIATION TIP: For a sweet version, omit the black pepper, lox, and dill and garnish instead with cinnamon sugar or fruit preserves.

Pear and Mango Compote with Honey

GLUTEN-FREE, KOSHER, VEGETARIAN / SERVES 6
PREP TIME: 10 minutes / **COOK TIME:** 30 minutes

Fragrant fruit compotes were part of the Ashkenazi culinary reper-toire in Europe, and today they make regular appearances at holiday meals or as side dishes. My light and refreshing version omits the typ-ical prunes and raisins in favor of lusciously sweet pears and mango (now a popular fruit in Israel). Serve alongside Cheese Blintzes with Blueberry Sauce (page 18) or Challah French Toast (page 17).

---

3 pears, peeled, cored, and sliced

1 mango, peeled, pitted, and cubed (about 1½ cups)

1 cup green grapes

¼ cup dried cranberries

½ tablespoon freshly squeezed lemon juice

1½ cups dry white wine, like Pinot Grigio

¼ cup honey

---

1. In a large saucepan over medium-high heat, combine the pears, mango, grapes, cranberries, lemon juice, wine, and honey. Add enough water to cover most of the fruit and bring to a boil.

2. Once boiling, reduce to a simmer and cook uncovered, stirring occasionally, until fruit is tender, about 20 minutes. Transfer only the fruit (not the liquid) to a bowl and set aside.

3. Return the remaining liquid to medium-high heat and boil until reduced by about half and slightly syrupy, about 10 minutes. Pour the syrup over the fruit and chill 6 hours or overnight. Refrigerate, covered, for up to 3 days.

INGREDIENT TIP: The white wine adds acidity and flavor, but you won't get buzzed eating this dish. After dilution with water and evaporation of more than half the wine's 5 to 14 percent alcohol content during cooking, very little alcohol remains in a serving. If preferred though, substitute non-alcoholic white wine or white grape juice.

Spicy Sabich with Roasted Eggplant

KOSHER, VEGETARIAN / SERVES 6
PREP TIME: 20 minutes / **COOK TIME:** 40 minutes

Sabich, introduced to Israel by way of Iraqi Jews, is a sandwich made by combining traditional Iraqi breakfast dishes in pita or laffa. Typical fillings include eggplant, Israeli chopped salad, tahini sauce or hummus, hard-boiled eggs, and a chutney or sauce, like zhug. Although the eggplant is typically fried, I prefer roasting it, which is easier and produces a deeper flavor.

---

2 medium eggplants

3 tablespoons extra-virgin olive oil, divided

1 tablespoon kosher salt, plus more to taste

2 tomatoes

1 small cucumber, peeled

½ teaspoon red wine vinegar

Freshly ground black pepper

6 small rounds Pita Bread (page 149) or other flatbread

6 hard-boiled eggs (ideally Huevos Haminados, page 28), sliced

½ cup Hummus (page 55)

Zhug (page 63) or harissa

---

1. Preheat the oven to 400°F. Line a sheet pan with foil.

2. Trim the eggplants into thick strips, about 4 inches long and ½ inch thick (like thick-cut fries).

3. Toss the eggplant slices with 2½ tablespoons olive oil to coat and sprinkle with 1 tablespoon of salt. Transfer to the sheet pan and roast about 30 minutes or until tender and lightly browned, turning once halfway through.

4. Meanwhile, chop the tomatoes and cucumber. Toss with the remaining ½ tablespoon olive oil, vinegar, and salt and pepper to taste.

5. Once the eggplant is done, warm the pitas in the oven at 350°F for about 10 minutes.

6. To assemble the sandwiches, halve and open the pitas. Spoon in the eggplant, tomato and cucumber salad, and eggs. Top with hummus and zhug or harissa to taste.

VARIATION TIP: Other ingredients to try: labneh, roasted or pickled vegetables, olives, crumbled feta, or tahini sauce.

✴ Huevos Haminados

GLUTEN-FREE, KOSHER, VEGETARIAN / SERVES 6
PREP TIME: 5 minutes / **COOK TIME:** 10 to 12 hours

When Sephardi Jews made overnight stews (hamin) for Shabbat, they nestled whole eggs in their shells into the pot to cook alongside the stew. The eggs emerged deeply browned, their insides laced with the flavor of the stew—faintly nutty with notes of bitter caramel. This slow-cooker version recreates this unique flavor. Serve plain, or in Spicy Sabich with Roasted Eggplant (page 26), during Passover.

12 eggs

1 cup black coffee

1 tablespoon red wine vinegar
  or white vinegar

1 teaspoon kosher salt

2 to 3 tablespoons extra-virgin
  olive oil

1. Place the unshelled eggs, coffee, vinegar, and salt in a slow cooker and add cool water to cover the eggs by at least one inch. Drizzle with olive oil.

2. Cover and cook on low for 10 to 12 hours (a longer cook time will yield deeper flavor).

3. Remove the eggs and cool in ice water, and discard the cooking liquid. Once cool enough to handle, peel and serve warm or at room temperature. Refrigerate leftover eggs for up to 5 days.

VARIATION TIP: To create marbled egg whites, remove the eggs 2 hours before done and gently crack the shells in several places. Return to the pot to finish cooking.

✳ Smoked Whitefish Salad

GLUTEN-FREE, KOSHER / SERVES 6
PREP TIME: 25 minutes, plus 3 hours chilling time

Smoked whitefish salads have long graced many a Shabbat break-fast table and Yom Kippur break-the-fast buffet. Whitefish entered the Jewish repertoire in Europe, where smoke-curing was a common preservation method. The flaky, smoky, and, delicate fish is perfect for creamy salads that go beautifully with bagels and crackers. Smoked whitefish is salted during curing, so you shouldn't need to add salt.

¼ cup mayonnaise

¼ cup sour cream

1 tablespoon chopped fresh dill

Freshly ground black pepper

1 pound smoked whitefish fillets, skinned, boned, and flaked

½ cup finely chopped celery

1 tablespoon minced sweet onion

¼ lemon

---

1. In a small bowl, combine the mayonnaise, sour cream, dill, and pepper to taste.

2. In a large bowl, gently combine the fish, celery, and onion. Stir in the dressing until the salad is just coated. Squeeze lemon over the salad and fold gently to incorporate.

3. Chill for at least 3 hours to let flavors develop. Adjust seasonings to taste before serving. Refrigerate, covered, for up to 2 days.

VARIATION TIP: For a dairy-free salad, replace the sour cream with additional mayonnaise.

Malawach (Yemenite Flaky Flatbread) with Grated Tomato

KOSHER, VEGETARIAN / SERVES 4 TO 6 (MAKES 8 FLATBREADS)
PREP TIME: 50 minutes, plus resting time / **COOK TIME:** 15 minutes

With just a few ingredients, this almost puff pastry–like flatbread is an irresistibly delicious hallmark of Yemenite Jewish cuisine, popular in Israel today. The skillet-cooked bread has multiple steps, but don't be intimidated—you'll get the hang of it. To make this dish quick for breakfast, roll the dough ahead of time (see recipe tip for storage).

---

4 cups all-purpose flour

1 tablespoon kosher salt, plus more
   for tomatoes

1 teaspoon sugar

1 cup warm water

1 stick unsalted butter, room
   temperature, cut into 10 chunks

2 large tomatoes

Freshly ground black pepper

---

1. In a large bowl, whisk together the flour, salt, and sugar. Slowly mix in the warm water, kneading until a mostly smooth, dense dough ball forms. If needed, add more water a teaspoon at a time.

2. Divide and roll the dough into 8 balls. Place them on a sheet pan lined with parchment paper, cover, and let rest at room temperature for 30 minutes.

3. Grease a smooth work surface with a chunk of butter. Place a dough ball on the buttered surface and roll it into a roughly 6-by-9-inch rectangle. Use your hands to continue pulling the dough until paper thin (small tears are okay), roughly 10 by 12 inches.

4. Rub a second chunk of butter over the dough. Roll the dough up from its long edge to form a rope. Coil the rope into a pinwheel (like a cinnamon roll) and return it to the sheet pan.

5. Repeat with the remaining dough balls, re-buttering the work surface frequently. Cover the coiled dough balls and refrigerate for 30 minutes.

6. Meanwhile, shred the tomatoes using the large holes on a box grater. Season with salt and pepper to taste. Set aside.

7. Remove the coiled dough from the refrigerator. Use your palm to flatten one coil, then place it between two sheets of wax paper and roll into a roughly 8-inch circle. Repeat with remaining dough.

8. Warm a medium nonstick skillet over medium heat. Once hot, fry the rounds, one at a time, until golden (1 to 2 minutes per side). Serve warm, topped with tomato.

MAKE AHEAD TIP: Once the dough is rolled into rounds (step 7), layer them between sheets of wax paper, place in a resealable bag, and freeze for up to a month. Fry directly from the freezer.

Chocolate "Egg Cream" Ice Cream Soda

GLUTEN-FREE, KOSHER, VEGETARIAN / SERVES 1
PREP TIME: 5 minutes

This soda fountain classic, which strangely contains neither eggs nor cream, dates back to New York City's Jewish neighborhoods in the 1890s, where its ice-cold creaminess was especially relished on hot summer days. It combines chocolate syrup and milk with an Eastern European Jewish favorite: seltzer. It's tough to recreate the soda-fountain foaminess of an egg cream at home, but this version made with chocolate gelato makes a festive and luscious treat for brunch and all day long.

2 tablespoons chocolate syrup
1 scoop chocolate gelato, slightly
   softened

½ cup plain seltzer, plus more
   to taste
Finely grated semisweet chocolate,
   for garnish (optional)

1. Drizzle the chocolate syrup into a tall glass. Add 1 scoop of chocolate gelato and stir to make a soft-serve texture.

2. Slowly fill the glass with seltzer, stirring vigorously to create a foamy top. Sprinkle with grated chocolate (if using). Serve immediately.

VARIATION TIP: For a grown-up version, make a bourbon "egg cream" float by mixing 1 to 2 tablespoons of bourbon into the chocolate syrup.

Classic Potato Latkes
Page 37

Chapter 3

Salads & Sides

EGGPLANT: THE MIGHTY AUBERGINE

If ever there were an essential Jewish fruit, the eggplant would be it. (Though we often treat it like a vegetable, it's technically a berry.) Jewish recipe collections often feature a wide variety of preparations with eggplant. Being able to cook eggplant multiple ways was legendarily a point of pride for Jewish cooks. You might find eggplant fried, roasted, mashed, stewed, stuffed, and even lightly sweetened or made into a jam.

Eggplants are native to southeast Asia and were cultivated in India for thousands of years. They entered Jewish cuisine around the ninth century after the fruit traveled west when Muslim rule expanded into Europe. Jews in Spain and Sicily especially prized eggplant for its meaty texture and versatility. Europeans later referred to it as the "Jewish apple."

So strong was the association that during the Spanish Inquisition, a preference for eggplant would raise the suspicions of inquisitors trying to root out Jews. After the Spanish expulsion in 1492, Sephardi and Sicilian Jews moved into Italy and beyond, carrying eggplant recipes with them. Thanks in part to this, the eggplant today shines in Jewish culinary traditions from the Mediterranean through North Africa.

Classic Potato Latkes

FAMILY-FRIENDLY, KOSHER, VEGETARIAN / SERVES 6 TO 8 (MAKES 18 TO 20 LATKES)
PREP TIME: 20 minutes / **COOK TIME:** 30 minutes

Latkes—fried potato pancakes—are a beloved Ashkenazi food, especially for Hanukkah. Long ago, cheese pancakes reigned for the holiday, but once potatoes became a staple of the Eastern European diet in the mid-1800s, crisp-tender potato pancakes served with sour cream or applesauce became the iconic favorite. Here's my classic take.

3 medium russet potatoes (about 2 pounds), peeled and shredded

1 large onion, shredded

2 large eggs

2 tablespoons all-purpose flour

2½ teaspoons kosher salt, or more to taste

¼ teaspoon ground black pepper

Vegetable oil for frying

Sour cream and Cinnamon-Spiced Applesauce (page 61), for serving (optional)

Chives for garnish (optional)

1. Combine the potatoes and onion in a fine mesh strainer. Press down on the mixture to drain excess liquid; then squeeze with a kitchen towel to wring out as much moisture as possible.

2. In a large bowl, whisk together the eggs, flour, salt, and pepper. Add the potato mixture and stir to incorporate.

3. In a large skillet over medium-high heat, warm about a ½-inch layer of vegetable oil. Form patties with about 2 tablespoons of potato mixture, and immediately slide them into the oil and flatten gently, working in batches to avoid crowding.

4. Cook 1 to 3 minutes per side, until deep golden brown all over. Transfer to a paper towel–lined plate and repeat with remaining mixture. Serve hot, with sour cream and applesauce, and garnish with chives, if using.

MAKE AHEAD TIP: Freeze cooked latkes for up to 1 month. To serve, bake from frozen at 350° F, on a wire rack set over a sheet pan, about 20 minutes.

Pickled Cucumber Salad

GLUTEN-FREE, KOSHER, VEGETARIAN / SERVES 6 TO 8 (MAKES 6 TO 7 CUPS)
PREP TIME: 15 minutes, plus resting time

This quick, refreshing salad comes from Hungarian and Polish Jewish origins and nods to the Eastern European tradition of pickling, especially of cucumbers. This quick-pickled salad can be eaten immediately or stored refrigerated (the flavors will meld over time).

---

2 large English cucumbers, sliced into ⅛-inch-thick rounds
½ small sweet onion, finely chopped
2 tablespoons white wine vinegar
1 tablespoon chopped fresh dill

¾ teaspoon kosher salt
Freshly ground black pepper
Pinch cayenne or red pepper flakes (optional)

---

1. In a large bowl, combine the cucumbers, onion, vinegar, dill, salt, and pepper to taste. Let rest for at least 30 minutes, stirring a few times. For a more pronounced pickled flavor, cover and chill for a few hours.

2. Serve at room temperature or chilled. Sprinkle with red pepper, if using. Refrigerate leftovers for up to 3 days.

VARIATION TIP: For a creamy version—also traditional—drain the liquid after resting or chilling and toss with ½ cup sour cream or enough to lightly coat.

Apple and Walnut Haroset

GLUTEN-FREE, KOSHER, VEGETARIAN / SERVES 8
PREP TIME: 15 minutes, plus 6 hours chilling time

Haroset is symbolic for Passover—the flavorful fruit-and-nut mixture represents the mortar used by Israelites enslaved in Egypt. (It tastes nothing like cement—I promise.) Classic Ashkenazi versions, like this one, use sweet fruit, wine, nuts, and warm spices. Honey is a traditional sweetener, but I find it's usually sweet enough without it.

---

3 cups shredded apples (such as Fuji or Honeycrisp), excess liquid lightly drained

1 cup walnuts, lightly toasted at 350°F (5 to 10 minutes) and finely chopped

1 teaspoon ground cinnamon

⅓ to ½ cup sweet wine, such as Manischewitz

1 to 2 tablespoons honey to sweeten (optional)

---

1. In a medium bowl, toss the apples and walnuts to combine. Stir in the cinnamon, then gradually add wine so the mixture is coated but not soupy. Add honey to taste, if using.

2. Cover and refrigerate until ready to serve, at least 6 hours.

3. Let stand at room temperature for 30 minutes before serving. Refrigerate leftovers for up to 3 days.

Date and Apricot Haroset Balls

FAMILY-FRIENDLY, GLUTEN-FREE, KOSHER, VEGETARIAN / SERVES 10 TO 12 (MAKES ABOUT 25 [1-INCH] BALLS)
PREP TIME: 15 minutes

Haroset recipes from North Africa and the Middle East often use warm spices and dried fruit, especially dates, which are native to the region and have symbolic significance in the Hebrew Bible. The dried fruit brings sweet, intense flavor and creates a sticky texture, making the haroset ideal for rolling into candy-like balls. They are festive for entertaining and simply fun to eat.

---

1 cup almonds

2 cups pitted dates, preferably Medjool

1 cup dried apricots

½ teaspoon cinnamon

¼ teaspoon nutmeg

¼ teaspoon salt

1 to 2 tablespoons sweet red wine

---

1. In a food processor, process the almonds until finely chopped, then add the dates and apricots and pulse until the mixture is well chopped with a sticky, clumpy texture.

2. Transfer to a bowl and stir in the cinnamon, nutmeg, salt, and 1 tablespoon of wine. Taste and add more wine as needed.

3. Shape tablespoonfuls of the mixture into 1-inch balls and place on a tray lined with wax paper. Serve at room temperature or store covered in the refrigerator for up to 3 days. (Return to room temperature before serving.)

VARIATION TIP: For a dressed-up presentation, roll the balls in shredded coconut.

Tabbouleh

KOSHER, VEGETARIAN / SERVES 4 TO 6
PREP TIME: 15 minutes, plus 25 minutes resting time

Parsley and mint are the stars of tabbouleh, which is popular all over the Middle East. Lebanese recipes use minimal bulgur, whereas this heftier version gained traction in Israel and the United States. No matter how much bulgur you use, though, tabbouleh's bright herbal flavor always shines through. To make gluten-free, Passover-friendly tabbouleh, substitute 3 to 4 cups of cooked quinoa for the bulgur.

1 cup fine bulgur

2 medium tomatoes, chopped

4 scallions, thinly sliced

1 cup flat-leaf parsley, chopped

1 cup fresh mint leaves, chopped

¼ cup freshly squeezed lemon juice

6 tablespoons extra-virgin olive oil

¼ teaspoon kosher salt, plus more to taste

Freshly ground black pepper

1. In a small bowl, combine the bulgur with boiling water to cover by about ½ inch. Let stand until bulgur is tender but still somewhat chewy, about 25 minutes. Drain any excess water.

2. Meanwhile, in a large bowl, combine the tomatoes, scallions, parsley, and mint.

3. To make the dressing, in a separate small bowl, whisk together the lemon juice, olive oil, salt, and pepper.

4. Add the bulgur to the parsley mixture. Toss gently with dressing just to coat (reserving excess). Let rest at room temperature for 10 to 30 minutes before serving or cover and chill overnight.

5. To serve, stir and add reserved dressing or seasonings to taste.

Israeli-Style Chopped Salad

GLUTEN-FREE, KOSHER, VEGETARIAN / SERVES 6 TO 8 (MAKES 6 TO 7 CUPS)
PREP TIME: 25 minutes

Mediterranean salads often highlight tomatoes and cucumbers, omitting lettuce. Israeli chopped salad is no exception. The colorful dish was a breakfast staple on Israel's working farms (kibbutzim), where workers adapted it from similar Sephardi and Mizrahi dishes. Today, it's standard at many meals. Enjoy plain or in Spicy Sabich with Roasted Eggplant (page 26), with Falafel (page 88), or with Malawach (page 30).

2 large or 3 medium English cucumbers, diced (but not peeled)

5 to 6 plum tomatoes, diced

1 green bell pepper, diced

1 yellow or orange bell pepper, diced

6 scallions, thinly sliced

2 tablespoons chopped flat-leaf parsley, plus more to taste

¼ cup extra-virgin olive oil

2 tablespoons freshly squeezed lemon juice

¾ teaspoon kosher salt

Freshly ground black pepper

1. In a large bowl, combine the cucumbers, tomatoes, bell pepper, scallion, and parsley.

2. To make the dressing, in a small bowl, whisk together the oil, lemon juice, salt, and pepper.

3. Toss the salad with the dressing to coat, and season to taste. Serve immediately.

VARIATION TIP: Add in crumbled feta and chickpeas for a heartier salad.

Artichokes, Jewish Style (Carciofi alla Giudia)

GLUTEN-FREE, KOSHER, VEGETARIAN / SERVES 4
PREP TIME: 25 minutes / **COOK TIME:** 20 minutes

Italian Jews developed their own cuisine, and their most famous dish, still found throughout Italy today, is deep-fried artichokes. Although they are often served whole, halving them makes preparation easier. To ensure crispy and delicate fried artichokes, thoroughly remove all the tough parts before frying.

4 medium to large artichokes	Kosher salt
Vegetable oil, for frying	

1. Prepare the artichokes. Cut the stem to about 1 inch and remove the dark leaves—about five layers' worth—until you reach pliable, light-green leaves. Cut off the top half of the leaves; then use a sharp knife to shave off leaf stubs around the base and the outer stem. Finally, halve the artichoke lengthwise and remove the thistly center leaves. Discard all trimmings.

2. Fill a large pot with a steamer basket with 2 inches of water and bring to a boil. Add the halved artichokes and steam, covered, until tender when pierced, 10 to 15 minutes. Remove and discard the fuzzy center chokes. Set steamed artichokes aside.

3. In a large Dutch oven on the stovetop, heat about 2 inches of oil to 350°F.

4. Once the oil is hot, tap the artichokes gently to separate their leaves. Gently drop four halves into the oil (being careful of spatters). Use tongs to submerge as fully as possible. Fry until browned and crisp, 3 to 6 minutes.

5. Remove to a paper towel–lined plate and repeat with the remaining halves.

6. Sprinkle with kosher salt to taste. Serve hot.

Maple, Carrot, and Sweet Potato Tzimmes

GLUTEN-FREE, KOSHER, VEGETARIAN / SERVES 6 TO 8
PREP TIME: 30 minutes / **COOK TIME:** 45 minutes

On Rosh Hashanah, the Jewish new year, many tables feature tzimmes—a slow-cooked stew made with dried fruit and root vegetables. Tzimmes has origins among Ashkenazi Jews in Germany and is also common on Passover, Sukkot, and Shabbat. Sliced carrot rounds represent gold coins, symbolizing hope for prosperity, but fruit represents sweetness. This modern version comes together faster and gets nuanced flavor from ginger, maple syrup, and a flaky sea salt.

---

3 tablespoons extra-virgin olive oil, plus more for greasing

1 pound carrots, peeled and cut into ¾-inch-thick rounds

3 medium sweet potatoes, peeled and cut into ¾-inch dice

1½ teaspoons kosher salt, divided

8 to 10 prunes, pitted and halved lengthwise

2 tablespoons maple syrup

½ tablespoon freshly squeezed lemon juice

½ teaspoon ground ginger

Freshly ground black pepper

¼ cup of water

Flaky sea salt, for serving (optional)

---

1. Preheat the oven to 375°F and grease a 9-by-9-inch casserole dish (or other 2-quart baking dish) with olive oil.

2. In a large saucepan over medium-high heat, combine the carrots, sweet potatoes, water to cover, and 1 teaspoon kosher salt and bring to a boil. Cook until the vegetables are softened but not fully tender, 10 to 15 minutes; then drain.

3. Toss the vegetables with the prunes, maple syrup, remaining 3 tablespoons of olive oil, lemon juice, ginger, remaining ½ teaspoon salt, and pepper to taste.

4. Transfer to the casserole dish, ensuring the prunes are spaced out on the top layer. Pour in ¼ cup of water.

 5. Cover the dish and bake for about 20 minutes; then uncover and roast for 10 to 15 more minutes, until tender. Sprinkle with sea salt, if using. Serve warm.

MAKE AHEAD TIP: Prepare the dish through step 4 and keep refrigerated for up to a day before baking (add 5 to 10 minutes to the covered baking time).

Caponata (Sicilian Eggplant with Tomatoes and Capers)

GLUTEN-FREE, KOSHER, VEGETARIAN / SERVES 6
PREP TIME: 15 minutes / **COOK TIME:** 45 minutes

Sicilian Jews, whose presence in Sicily dates back possibly 2,000 years, adopted eggplant early on when it arrived by way of trade or Muslim conquest. Thus emerged caponata, an enduringly loved dish starring cooked eggplant and other local ingredients. Caponata is preserved using vinegar and sugar, making it suitable for Shabbat in the days before modern refrigeration. In my version, the eggplant is roasted and sautéed with colorful peppers. Serve as a side dish with toasted bread or use as a pasta sauce.

2 medium eggplants (approximately 2 pounds), cut into 1-inch cubes

Extra-virgin olive oil

Kosher salt

1 large onion, coarsely chopped

2 bell peppers (1 red, 1 yellow), chopped into roughly 1-inch pieces

½ cup chopped celery (¼- to ½-inch pieces)

Freshly ground black pepper

3 garlic cloves, crushed or minced

1 (14.5 ounce) can diced tomatoes with juices

1 tablespoon capers, drained

1 tablespoon sugar

1 tablespoon red wine vinegar

1. Preheat the oven to 475°F and line two rimmed sheet pans with nonstick aluminum foil.

2. Spread eggplant in a single layer on the sheet pans. Toss with oil to lightly coat and season generously with salt. Roast for 20 to 30 minutes, stirring a few times throughout, until browned and tender. Set aside.

3. Heat a thin layer of oil in a Dutch oven or other deep-sided pan over medium-high heat. Add the onion, bell peppers, and celery and season lightly with salt and pepper to taste. Sauté until the vegetables begin to soften, 6 to 10 minutes.

4. Add the garlic and cook for about 30 seconds. Stir in the tomatoes, eggplant, capers, sugar, and vinegar. Adjust heat to low and simmer for 5 to 10 minutes, until the mixture is thick and vegetables are tender but not mushy.

5. Season to taste and serve warm or at room temperature. Refrigerate leftovers covered for up to 5 days.

Moroccan Orange and Black Olive Salad

GLUTEN-FREE, KOSHER, VEGETARIAN / SERVES 4 TO 6
PREP TIME: 10 minutes, plus 30 minutes resting time

Oranges thrive in the Mediterranean, and early Jewish communities in the region were heavily involved in growing them, according to the late food historian Gil Marks. Naturally, the orange is used in many Sephardi dishes, like this salad, versions of which are popular throughout Morocco. It combines sweet, salty, and spicy flavors in a spectacular, aromatic presentation—especially when oranges are at peak season. For best flavor, chill a few hours before serving.

---

6 small to medium assorted oranges (such as navel, Cara Cara, and blood oranges)

¾ cup pitted black olives (preferably oil cured)

¼ cup extra-virgin olive oil

¼ cup freshly squeezed lemon juice (about 1½ lemons)

1 teaspoon cumin

¾ teaspoon cinnamon

¼ teaspoon red pepper flakes, minced

Kosher salt

Freshly ground black pepper

---

1. Peel the oranges, removing as much pith as possible. Slice them crosswise (into ¼- to ½-inch-thick rounds, or as desired) and place in a large bowl with the olives.

2. In a small bowl, make the dressing by whisking together the oil, juice, cumin, cinnamon, red pepper flakes, and salt and pepper to taste.

3. Gently toss the oranges and olives with just enough dressing to coat, reserving the rest. Let the salad rest at room temperature for at least 30 minutes to let flavors develop, stirring once or twice, or chill a few hours.

4. Adjust seasonings or dressing to taste. Serve at room temperature or chilled. Refrigerate leftovers for up to 3 days.

INGREDIENT TIP: Oil-cured black olives are dry cured in salt and then macerated in oil, giving them a shriveled appearance, meaty texture, and enhanced flavor. For this dish, avoid olives packed in seasoned oils.

Spinach with Raisins and Pine Nuts

GLUTEN-FREE, KOSHER, VEGETARIAN / SERVES 4 TO 6
PREP TIME: 10 minutes / **COOK TIME:** 10 minutes

When Muslim rulers arrived in the Iberian peninsula and Sicily during the ninth century, they introduced the combination of raisins or currants and pine nuts, often cooked with spinach. Later, Sicilian and Sephardi Jews likely carried this preparation north, where it became a specialty in Rome and Venice, and after that in Greece, Turkey, and Spain. It's a venerable side dish for Shabbat dinners and on Rosh Hashanah.

¼ cup raisins, golden raisins, or currants

Extra-virgin olive oil

1 small sweet onion, finely chopped

3 tablespoons pine nuts

3 garlic cloves, slivered

3 (8-ounce) bags prewashed spinach (not baby spinach)

¼ lemon, plus additional as needed

Kosher salt

Freshly ground black pepper

---

1. Add the raisins to a small bowl and cover with hot water. Let rest until plump, about 10 minutes, and drain.

2. Meanwhile, warm a thin layer of olive oil in a large skillet over low heat. Once hot, fry the onion until softened, 3 to 5 minutes. Add the pine nuts and garlic and stir until lightly browned, 1 to 3 minutes.

3. Increase heat slightly. Add half the spinach, turning constantly, and after it starts to wilt, add the rest. Cook, stirring frequently, until wilted and most liquid is evaporated, 3 to 5 minutes.

4. Squeeze lemon juice over the top and stir in the raisins, salt, and pepper.

5. If bitter, add more lemon juice to taste. Transfer to a bowl (drain excess liquid if desired). Serve warm or at room temperature.

Roasted Pepper Salad

GLUTEN-FREE, KOSHER, VEGETARIAN / SERVES 4
PREP TIME: 15 minutes, plus resting time / **COOK TIME:** 30 minutes

Roasted peppers appeared frequently on Jewish tables throughout the Mediterranean, in mezzes—a collection of small appetizers—as well as salads. Different regions combined distinctive ingredients with the peppers, such as anchovies in Italy, tomato sauce and chili paste in Yemen, and garlic and hot pepper in Tunisia (used in this recipe). In this version, every bite packs robust flavor, so small servings go a long way.

---

5 assorted bell peppers (red, yellow, and orange), halved and seeded

1 to 2 hot red chiles, halved and seeded (optional)

Extra-virgin olive oil

1 medium onion, finely chopped

Kosher salt

Freshly ground black pepper

3 garlic cloves, minced

½ tablespoon red wine vinegar

---

1. Preheat your oven's broiler on high and line 2 sheet pans with aluminum foil.

2. Place the peppers (and chiles, if using), cut-side down, on the sheet pans and lightly coat the tops with oil. Broil until skins are mostly blackened, 15 to 25 minutes.

3. Remove and carefully wrap the peppers in the foil from the sheet pan to seal so steam doesn't escape. Cool for at least 15 minutes.

4. Peel and discard the pepper skins. Slice peppers into ribbons and place in a bowl with their cooking juices.

5. Warm a thin layer of oil in a medium nonstick skillet over medium-high heat. Add the onion and salt and pepper to taste. Cook until softened, stirring frequently, 3 to 5 minutes. Add the garlic and stir constantly until fragrant, about 1 minute.

6. Combine the onion and pepper mixtures, drizzle with vinegar, and season to taste. Serve warm or at room temperature. Refrigerate leftovers covered for up to 3 days.

Matzah Ball Soup
Page 68

Chapter 4

Spreads & Soups

CHICKEN SOUP: A PRICELESS POT OF GOLD

Jewish chicken soup, *goldene yoich* (in Yiddish, "golden broth"), is legendary. Although Jews weren't the first to make it, they've done a lot to celebrate and popularize it. Picking up on Chinese observations of the simple soup's medicinal and healing qualities, the twelfth-century Jewish scholar (and doctor) Moses Maimonides recommended chicken soup for anyone feeling weak or sick and for women who had just given birth. We have him in large part to thank for the concept of chicken soup as "Jewish Penicillin."

Sephardi and Mizrahi Jews have made versions of chicken soup since at least medieval times. Once chickens became more widely available in Europe in the fifteenth century, chicken soup took off in Ashkenazi Jewish communities, becoming a Sabbath, holiday, and wedding staple served with noodles, kreplach, and matzah balls. The love affair continued when Ashkenazi immigrants arrived in America.

Although the basic approach remains similar, recipes vary among cultures. For example, Persian versions include turmeric and chickpea dumplings, and Indian versions often feature ginger and cardamom. According to food historian Joan Nathan, Yemenite Jews might have the oldest chicken soup recipe in existence—their spicy version includes garlic, fenugreek, and chiles. No matter how it's made, chicken soup is a humble basic that reigns as one of Jewish cuisine's greatest culinary riches.

Hummus

GLUTEN-FREE, KOSHER, VEGETARIAN / SERVES 6
PREP TIME: 15 minutes

Long before hummus became a ubiquitous food in Israel and around the world, cooks across the Middle East and North Africa were making it with fava beans or chickpeas as part of mezzes. Its origins remain hotly debated, but the first known mention of it appears in a cookbook from thirteenth-century Cairo. Hummus is easy to prepare at home, especially using canned beans. Of countless variations, this basic version remains my favorite. Serve with Pita Bread (page 149) or vegetable sticks.

1 (15.5-ounce) can chickpeas, drained with liquid reserved
⅓ cup tahini
2½ tablespoons freshly squeezed lemon juice
1 to 2 garlic cloves

¼ teaspoon cumin
¼ teaspoon kosher salt
Freshly ground black pepper
2 tablespoons pine nuts, for garnish
Paprika, for garnish
Extra-virgin olive oil, for garnish

1. In a blender, process the chickpeas, tahini, lemon juice, garlic, cumin, salt, pepper, and ⅓ cup of the reserved chickpea liquid. Continue processing, adding chickpea liquid as needed until smooth and creamy. Season to taste and chill, covered, until ready to serve.

2. Toast the pine nuts in a small skillet over medium heat, stirring frequently, 5 to 7 minutes or until lightly browned.

3. To serve, spoon the hummus into a wide, flat bowl, making a slight indent in the center. Sprinkle with paprika, drizzle olive oil into the indent, and top with pine nuts.

STORAGE TIP: Refrigerate hummus for up to 4 days. (It also freezes well.)

✴ Baba Ghanoush

GLUTEN-FREE, KOSHER, VEGETARIAN / SERVES 4 TO 6 (MAKES 1½ CUPS)
PREP TIME: 10 minutes / **COOK TIME:** 40 minutes, plus resting time

Eggplant was cooked in many ways across the Mediterranean and Middle East, but among the most popular preparations (among Jews and non-Jews alike) were mashed eggplant spreads like baba ghanoush. Israeli Jews adopted baba ghanoush from neighboring countries, and today it's a favorite, served with bread or sliced vegetables. Use smaller eggplants for better flavor and fewer seeds.

---

2 small eggplants, or 1 large eggplant
  (1½ to 2 pounds)
2 garlic cloves, or more to taste, unpeeled
Extra-virgin olive oil
3 tablespoons tahini
1 tablespoon freshly squeezed
  lemon juice

¾ teaspoon kosher salt, plus more
  to taste
Freshly ground black pepper
Pinch cayenne pepper (optional)
Chopped parsley, for garnish (optional)

---

1. Preheat your oven's broiler on high and line a rimmed sheet pan with aluminum foil.

2. Rub the eggplants and garlic with olive oil and poke eggplants all over with a knife or fork to allow steam to escape.

3. Place eggplants and garlic on the sheet pan and broil. Remove the garlic once tender, about 6 minutes. Continue broiling the eggplants until charred and shriveled, about 40 minutes, turning occasionally. Cool about 15 minutes.

4. Peel the garlic and eggplant and discard the skins. Transfer the flesh to a large bowl and drain excess liquid.

5. Add in the tahini, lemon juice, salt, and pepper to taste. Mash the mixture with a fork or use an immersion blender to puree until mostly smooth. Season to taste and add cayenne pepper, if using.

 6. Let rest for 30 minutes, or refrigerate for a few hours for optimal flavor before serving. Garnish with parsley, if using, just before serving.

STORAGE TIP: Refrigerate covered for up to 3 days.

Muhammara (Roasted Red Pepper and Walnut Spread)

KOSHER, VEGETARIAN / SERVES 4 TO 6 (MAKES 1¼ CUPS)
PREP TIME: 10 minutes / **COOK TIME:** 25 minutes

Colorful bell peppers have long been favorites for mezzes and savored in spreads like this one of Turkish and Syrian origins. Here, roasted peppers create rich texture and flavor, accentuated by the typical ingredients of walnuts, breadcrumbs, and pomegranate molasses. Use as a dip for bread or vegetables, or as a condiment.

---

4 red bell peppers, halved lengthwise and seeded

4 tablespoons extra-virgin olive oil, divided, plus more as needed

1 cup walnuts

⅓ cup panko breadcrumbs

1 garlic clove, unpeeled

¼ teaspoon red pepper flakes, minced

2 tablespoons pomegranate molasses

1 teaspoon sugar

¼ teaspoon kosher salt, plus more to taste

---

1. Preheat the broiler to high and line two sheet pans with aluminum foil.

2. Place the peppers cut-side down on the sheet pans and coat the tops with 2 tablespoons of the oil. Broil the peppers until the skins are mostly blackened, 15 to 25 minutes.

3. Remove from the oven and wrap the foil around the peppers to prevent steam from escaping. Cool for 15 minutes.

4. Meanwhile, heat a medium skillet over medium heat. Toast the walnuts, shaking the pan frequently, until fragrant and just starting to brown, about 4 minutes. Remove from the pan and set aside.

5. In the same pan, toast the garlic clove until lightly browned and fragrant, about 2 minutes. Peel once cooled.

6. Once the peppers are cool enough to handle, peel and discard the skins.

7. In a small food processor, blend the peppers, walnuts, breadcrumbs, garlic, red pepper flakes, pomegranate molasses, sugar, salt, and the remaining 2 tablespoons of olive oil. Blend until a chunky paste forms, adding more oil as needed.

8. Season to taste. Serve immediately or cover and refrigerate for up to 3 days.

SUBSTITUTION TIP: If you can't find pomegranate molasses, substitute honey or agave mixed with balsamic vinegar or lemon juice.

✳ Beet Horseradish

GLUTEN-FREE, KOSHER, VEGETARIAN / MAKES ½ CUP
PREP TIME: 15 minutes / **COOK TIME:** 40 minutes

Native to Eastern Europe, horseradish was adopted as the "bitter herb" on the Passover Seder plate, despite being neither bitter nor an herb. Eastern European Jews also found that pungent chrain (horseradish paste) was an ideal complement for mild gefilte fish. Here, beets add vibrant color and help mellow the bite—but a small spoonful still goes a long way.

---

1 small beet, peeled

1 5-inch piece fresh horseradish root (about ½ pound), peeled

¼ teaspoon kosher salt

¼ teaspoon sugar

½ tablespoon white vinegar

---

1. In a medium saucepan, cover the beet with lightly salted water. Place over medium heat and simmer about 30 minutes, until tender. Drain.

2. Using the small holes of a box grater (or by placing 1-inch chunks in a food processor), finely grate the beet and horseradish. Transfer the mixture to a bowl and add the salt, sugar, and vinegar, stirring to incorporate.

3. Serve immediately, or cover and refrigerate for up to 5 days.

Cinnamon-Spiced Applesauce

FAMILY-FRIENDLY, GLUTEN-FREE, KOSHER, VEGETARIAN / SERVES 4 (MAKES 4 CUPS)
PREP TIME: 10 minutes / **COOK TIME:** 15 minutes, plus 4 hours chilling time

Apples feature in dishes for many Jewish holidays—they symbolize a sweet new year on Rosh Hashanah and are used in many Passover harosets. On Hanukkah, applesauce is served as a condiment for latkes—but it makes a fresh, palate-pleasing side dish almost anytime. This applesauce is easy to make and far superior to anything store-bought. Since apples vary in sweetness, be sure to taste after cooking and adjust sugar and cinnamon to your preference.

3 to 4 large apples (about 3 pounds), such as Honeycrisp, peeled and coarsely chopped
1½ cups of water
1 tablespoon honey
½ tablespoon freshly squeezed lemon juice

3 teaspoons light brown sugar, plus more to taste
3 cinnamon sticks
½ teaspoon ground cinnamon, plus more to taste

1. In a medium saucepan, combine the apples, water, honey, lemon juice, brown sugar, and cinnamon sticks.

2. Bring to a simmer, cover, and cook for 10 to 15 minutes, until the apples are tender.

3. Remove from the heat and discard the cinnamon sticks. Use a potato masher or immersion blender to mash the applesauce to your preferred smoothness.

4. Stir in the ground cinnamon. Taste for seasoning, noting that flavors will intensify once chilled. Cover and chill at least 4 hours or overnight before serving.

Chopped Liver

GLUTEN-FREE / SERVES 6 TO 8
PREP TIME: 15 minutes / **COOK TIME:** 25 minutes, plus 2 hours chilling time

In Ashkenazi tradition, chopped liver on bread or crackers has been a Shabbat and holiday appetizer for centuries. This modest update brightens flavor with olive oil, a splash of vinegar, and a flaky sea salt garnish. For a traditional chunky texture, chop the ingredients by hand.

Extra-virgin olive oil

2 large yellow onions, sliced

Kosher salt

Freshly ground black pepper

1 tablespoon apple cider vinegar or dry white wine

1 pound chicken livers, rinsed, patted dry, membranes and veins removed

4 hard-boiled eggs, peeled and chopped, ¼ reserved for garnish

Flaky sea salt (optional)

1. Warm a layer of oil in a large skillet over medium-low heat. Add the onion and season with salt and pepper to taste. Toss to coat, cover, and cook until softened, about 10 minutes.

2. Adjust heat to low, uncover, and cook the onion until deep golden brown, about 10 more minutes, stirring occasionally. Stir in the vinegar and transfer the mixture to a food processor or bowl. Set aside.

3. Add the livers to the skillet in a single layer, adding oil as needed and seasoning with salt and pepper to taste. Fry until lightly browned and cooked through, about 3 minutes per side. Transfer to a food processor.

4. Process or chop the mixture until it reaches your desired consistency. Fold in ¾ of the eggs, adding oil as needed to achieve desired consistency. Cover and chill at least two hours or overnight.

5. To serve, season to taste, and top with the remaining egg and flaky salt.

KOSHER TIP: Livers contain a lot of blood and must be handled a specific way to be kosher. Please consult your trusted authority for guidance.

Zhug (Yemenite Green Chile Paste)

GLUTEN-FREE, KOSHER, VEGETARIAN / MAKES ¾ CUP
PREP TIME: 15 minutes

Devotees of this fresh, herbal, fiery paste put it on everything—bread, salads, grilled meat, soups, and more. Yemenite Jews first brought the sauce—which features cilantro, chiles, and cumin—to Israel in the early twentieth century. Today it's become something of a national condiment. Serve with Falafel (page 88), in Pita Bread (page 149), or with Yemenite Beef Soup (page 72).

---

2 cups lightly packed fresh Italian parsley (leaves and fine stems)

2 cups lightly packed fresh cilantro (leaves and fine stems)

2 to 4 hot peppers, such as jalapeños or serrano peppers, halved, seeded, and pith removed

2 garlic cloves

½ teaspoon ground cumin

½ teaspoon ground cardamom

¼ teaspoon ground cloves

½ teaspoon kosher salt

Freshly ground black pepper

½ cup extra-virgin olive oil, plus more as needed

---

1. In a food processor or blender, combine the parsley, cilantro, hot peppers, garlic, cumin, cardamom, cloves, salt, and pepper to taste. Drizzle in oil to form a thick, coarse paste, slowly adding more as needed to thin. Season to taste.

2. Keep refrigerated in an airtight jar for up to 5 days. If paste gets too thick, stir in a little warm water.

INGREDIENT TIP: If raw garlic is too pungent for your taste, lightly toast the cloves before adding them to the mixture. And if the sauce seems bitter, add a squeeze of lemon or lime juice or a pinch of sugar.

Garlic and Za'atar Labneh

GLUTEN-FREE, KOSHER, VEGETARIAN / SERVES 6
PREP TIME: 10 minutes / **COOK TIME:** 8 minutes

Many Middle Eastern mezzes feature labneh, a thick and tangy drained yogurt, topped with various seasonings. A common topping is za'atar, a spice blend widely popular in Israel and now available at many major supermarkets in the United States. In this recipe, za'atar, chives, and toasted garlic transform labneh into a palate-pleasing, super-quick dip for Pita Bread (page 149) or sliced vegetables.

3 large garlic cloves, unpeeled

1 cup labneh

2 tablespoons finely chopped fresh chives

¼ teaspoon kosher salt

Freshly ground black pepper

1 tablespoon extra-virgin olive oil

1 teaspoon za'atar

1. In a small skillet over medium heat, toast the garlic for 5 to 10 minutes or until lightly browned, turning occasionally. Remove, squeeze the pulp from the skins, and mince.

2. In a medium bowl, combine the labneh, chives, garlic, salt, and pepper to taste. Add water a few drops at a time as needed to thin.

3. Spoon the labneh mixture into a small bowl and smooth. Drizzle with olive oil and sprinkle with za'atar.

PREPARATION TIP: If using a food processor, pulse only a few times, or the mixture might become runny.

Moroccan Lentil Soup (Harira)

KOSHER, VEGETARIAN / SERVES 8 TO 10
PREP TIME: 15 minutes / **COOK TIME:** 45 minutes

Harira—a silky, hearty soup—originated in Morocco, where Muslims serve it to break the fast on Ramadan; Moroccan Jews adopted it as well. This vegetarian version features the customary chickpeas, lentils, and cumin, and is vibrant in flavor and color, with a golden-hued broth flecked with tomatoes and parsley.

Extra-virgin olive oil
2 large onions, chopped
1 cup chopped celery
Kosher salt
Freshly ground black pepper
1 teaspoon ground cumin
¾ teaspoon ground turmeric
Cayenne pepper (optional)

1 (14.5-ounce) can diced tomatoes with juices
1 (15.5-ounce) can chickpeas, drained
1 cup uncooked brown lentils
6 cups vegetable stock
⅓ cup all-purpose flour
¼ cup cool water
½ cup chopped flat-leaf parsley

---

1. Warm a layer of oil in a large soup pot over medium heat. Add the onion and celery and season with salt and pepper to taste. Cook until softened, about 5 minutes, stirring frequently.

2. Stir in the cumin, turmeric, and a pinch of cayenne pepper (if using). Add the tomatoes, chickpeas, lentils, and stock. Bring to a boil, then reduce the heat to low and simmer for 15 minutes.

3. Stir together the flour and cool water to make a slurry. Slowly pour the slurry into the soup, stirring constantly. Simmer 15 more minutes, until the chickpeas and lentils are tender.

4. Remove from the heat and stir in the parsley. Season to taste and serve hot.

VARIATION TIP: Make this dish heartier by adding thin noodles, like vermicelli, during the last 10 to 15 minutes of cooking.

Classic Chicken Soup

FAMILY-FRIENDLY, GLUTEN-FREE, KOSHER / SERVES 8 TO 10
PREP TIME: 20 minutes / **COOK TIME:** 3 hours

The aroma of chicken soup cooking on the stove signals family, home, and holiday for many Jews—and just about everyone. Many people have special family recipes, but the basic idea remains deliciously the same. Gently cook chicken, aromatics, and water for a few hours and you've got culinary gold. Use this recipe for Matzah Ball Soup (page 68).

---

2 large onions, cut into large pieces

3 ribs of celery with leaves, cut into large pieces

3 large carrots, cut into large pieces

3 bay leaves

1 sprig fresh rosemary

¾ cup loosely packed fresh dill, plus more for optional garnish

2 to 3 sprigs flat-leaf parsley

1 teaspoon whole black peppercorns

1 4-pound whole chicken, cut into 4 or 8 pieces

1 pound chicken drumsticks

Kosher salt

---

1. In a large soup pot, combine the onion, celery, carrot, bay leaves, rosemary, ¾ cup of dill, parsley, peppercorns, and chicken (including the additional drumsticks). Cover just barely with cold water.

2. Bring to a gentle boil over medium-low heat, skimming off any foam from the surface. Once boiling, cover loosely and simmer for 40 minutes.

3. Remove half of the carrots, celery, and white meat chicken to save for serving. Thinly slice the carrots and celery and shred the white meat from the bones. Chill, covered, until serving. Return chicken bones and scraps to the pot.

4. Cook the soup for 1½ more hours, then turn the heat to high and boil for 15 minutes to concentrate the flavor.

5. Strain the liquid, discard the solids, and clean out the pot. Return the liquid to the pot and bring to a boil.

6. Return the reserved carrot, celery, and chicken to the pot and cook for 5 minutes. Season with salt and pepper to taste.

7. Serve the soup with noodles or rice, or use in Matzah Ball Soup (page 68). Garnish with chopped dill, if using.

> **MAKE AHEAD TIP:** To freeze the stock, cool the strained liquid and chill overnight. The next day, remove the accumulated fat and freeze.

Matzah Ball Soup

FAMILY-FRIENDLY, KOSHER / SERVES 6 TO 8 (MAKES 20 TO 25 BALLS)
PREP TIME: 30 minutes, plus 40 minutes chilling time / **COOK TIME:** 30 minutes

The matzah ball is an icon of Jewish cooking, but it has humble beginnings—it emerged when Ashkenazi cooks used matzah meal instead of flour to make kosher-for-Passover dumplings (knaidlach). Today, matzah ball soup plays a starring role at many Passover feasts and year-round at Jewish delis as an ultimate comfort food. Using schmaltz (chicken fat) is traditional, but olive oil works beautifully—and is healthier—for this fluffy-but-still-firm recipe.

1⅓ cups matzah meal

½ tablespoon salt

¼ teaspoon freshly ground black pepper

5 large eggs, beaten until uniformly colored

¼ cup extra-virgin olive oil

¼ cup chicken broth or water

1½ tablespoons finely chopped chives

¼ cup seltzer water

Classic Chicken Soup (page 66) or 2 quarts store-bought chicken broth

Chopped flat-leaf parsley or dill for garnish, optional

---

1. In a large bowl, combine the matzah meal, salt, and pepper. Add the eggs, olive oil, broth or water, and chives. Fold in seltzer water. Freeze the mixture for 30 minutes.

2. With wet hands, shape the mixture into 1¼-inch balls and place on a plate or tray. Return to the freezer for 10 minutes.

3. Meanwhile, bring a large pot of salted water to boil over medium-high heat.

4. Once boiling, drop the balls into the water. Cover and boil gently for 30 minutes, until puffy and evenly colored. Using a slotted spoon, remove from the water until ready to serve.

5. Serve in individual bowls and add hot Classic Chicken Soup or broth. Garnish with parsley or dill, if using.

SUBSTITUTION TIP: The chives can be substituted with finely chopped dill or flat-leaf parsley, or ⅛ teaspoon ground nutmeg, ginger, or garlic powder.

Mushroom-Barley Soup

KOSHER / SERVES 8 TO 10
PREP TIME: 30 minutes / **COOK TIME:** 1 hour 15 minutes

Creamy, hearty mushroom-barley soup (also known as krupnik) was originally commonplace in Poland, Lithuania, and Ukraine. Ashkenazi Jews brought it to America, where it became a comforting regular at delis and at home. Some versions include meat, but this one lets mushrooms do the work, with a little help from the modern addition of Worcestershire sauce.

---

1 ounce dried porcini mushrooms

1 cup boiling water

Extra-virgin olive oil

1 large onion, chopped

2 ribs celery, finely chopped

2 medium carrots, finely chopped

Kosher salt

Freshly ground black pepper

1 pound mixed fresh mushrooms (preferably shiitake and cremini), chopped into roughly ½-inch pieces

4 garlic cloves, minced

8 cups water

1 tablespoon Worcestershire sauce

½ cup pearl barley

---

1. In a small bowl, cover the dried porcini mushrooms in the boiling water. Let stand 10 minutes. Strain through a coffee filter, reserving the liquid. Rinse and chop the rehydrated mushrooms.

2. Heat a layer of oil in a large soup pot over medium heat. Add the onion, celery, and carrot. Season lightly with salt and pepper to taste. Cook until softened, stirring frequently, about 8 minutes.

3. Add in the fresh mushrooms and rehydrated porcinis. Season with salt and pepper to taste and cook until mushrooms soften, about 5 minutes. Stir in the garlic and cook, stirring constantly, 1 minute.

4. Add the 8 cups of water, the reserved mushroom liquid, Worcestershire sauce, and barley. Adjust the heat to medium-high and bring to a boil.

5. Reduce the heat to low, and simmer partially covered, 50 to 60 minutes or until the barley is tender, stirring occasionally. Season to taste and serve hot.

KOSHER TIP: For kosher observance with a meat meal, note that Worcestershire sauce contains anchovies but can be substituted with soy sauce.

Yemenite Beef Soup

GLUTEN-FREE, KOSHER / SERVES 6 TO 8 (MAKES ABOUT 8 CUPS)
PREP TIME: 20 minutes / **COOK TIME:** 2 hours

For a fragrantly spiced and wonderfully filling soup, turn to this beef version from Yemenite Jewish cuisine. Commonly prepared for Shabbat, the soup gets flavor from generous amounts of cumin, turmeric, cardamom, and black pepper (often blended in the traditional spice mixture called hawaij). Serve topped with a spoonful of Zhug (page 63) and bread for dipping.

Extra-virgin olive oil

1 pound beef chuck or stew beef, cut into 1-inch chunks

Kosher salt

Freshly ground black pepper

2 large onions, chopped

6 cloves garlic, slivered

2 teaspoons ground cumin

1 teaspoon ground cardamom

2 teaspoons ground turmeric

3 tablespoons tomato paste

7 cups beef stock or water

4 Yukon Gold potatoes (about 1 pound), peeled and cut into 1-inch cubes

½ cup chopped cilantro

---

1. Heat a thin layer of oil in a large Dutch oven over medium-high heat. Add the meat, seasoning with salt and pepper to taste. Cook, turning occasionally, until browned, about 8 minutes. Remove and set aside.

2. Add in the onion and season lightly with salt and pepper. Cook until softened, about 5 minutes, stirring frequently. Add the garlic, cumin, cardamom, and turmeric and cook until fragrant, about 2 minutes, stirring constantly.

3. Return the meat to the pot, stir in the tomato paste, and add the stock or water. Bring to a boil, then reduce heat to a low simmer, skimming off any foam that rises to the top. Cover partially and cook until the meat is tender, about 1½ hours.

4. Add the potatoes to the soup and simmer, uncovered, for 15 to 20 minutes or until tender. Remove from the heat, taste for seasoning, and add the cilantro.

> **MAKE AHEAD TIP:** Make soup as directed, adding only half the cilantro and reserving ¼ cup. Refrigerate the soup overnight and reheat it the next day, adding the remaining cilantro just before serving.

Borscht (Beet Soup with Sour Cream)

GLUTEN-FREE, KOSHER, VEGETARIAN / SERVES 10 TO 12 (MAKES 11 CUPS)
PREP TIME: 15 minutes / **COOK TIME:** 45 minutes

Jewel-toned, sweet-and-sour beet soup was likely adopted by Ashkenazi Jews in what are now Russia, Ukraine, and Lithuania. Its popularity soared in America so much that borscht became commercially produced in jars. Meat-based borscht is served hot, but vegetarian borscht (like this recipe) can be served hot or cold, with sour cream added as desired.

6 to 8 medium beets, peeled and quartered

1 large onion, finely chopped

8 cups of water

1½ tablespoons sugar

3 tablespoons freshly squeezed lemon juice

¾ teaspoon kosher salt, plus more to taste

Freshly ground black pepper

Sour cream, for garnish

1. In a large soup pot, combine the beets, onion, and water. Bring to a boil, then cover and reduce the heat. Simmer until the beets are tender, about 40 minutes.

2. Stir in the sugar, lemon juice, salt, and pepper to taste. Simmer 5 more minutes.

3. Remove from the heat and puree the soup using an immersion blender or in batches in a blender.

4. Serve hot or, to serve cold, chill for 8 hours or overnight. Garnish with sour cream.

VARIATION TIP: If you like partly-chunky borscht, remove 6 to 8 beet pieces before pureeing. Set aside to cool, then dice and add back to the pureed soup.

Roasted Butternut Squash Soup

GLUTEN-FREE / SERVES 6
PREP TIME: 15 minutes / **COOK TIME:** 50 minutes

Long ago, meaty-fleshed winter squash—close in flavor to today's butternut squash—made its way into Jewish soups, hand pies, purees, and rice dishes worldwide, in part by way of Sephardi Jews migrating from the Iberian Peninsula. Today, silky, rich butternut squash soup has become a popular addition to Shabbat dinners and Jewish holiday dinners in autumn.

---

2 (12-ounce) containers (about 6 to 7 cups) pre-cut butternut squash cubes

2 cups quartered shallots

2 tablespoons light brown sugar

1½ teaspoons kosher salt

Freshly ground black pepper

Extra-virgin olive oil

2 teaspoons finely grated fresh ginger

4 cups chicken or vegetable broth, divided

¾ cup shredded fontina cheese, for garnish (optional)

---

1. Preheat the oven to 450°F and line a large sheet pan with aluminum foil.

2. Combine the squash, shallots, sugar, salt, and pepper to taste directly on the sheet pan. Lightly coat with oil and spread in a single layer. Roast until tender, 25 to 35 minutes, turning occasionally.

3. In a large pot, warm a layer of oil over medium heat. Add the ginger and sauté for 1 minute, stirring constantly. Add 3½ cups of broth, along with the roasted vegetables and their juices. Bring to a boil, then reduce heat to low and simmer for 10 minutes, or until the vegetables are very tender. Puree with an immersion blender or in batches in a blender. Add the remaining broth or water as needed to reach desired consistency.

4. Season to taste and serve hot, sprinkled with cheese (if using).

KOSHER TIP: Omit the cheese if using chicken broth.

Falafel
Page 88

Vegetarian Mains

MATZAH: THE 18-MINUTE MIRACLE

In any Jewish tradition, there's one thing you'll always find: matzah. Though short on flavor, this unleavened "loaf" carries a lot of historical weight on its brittle frame. Matzah commemorates the exodus from Egypt, when enslaved Israelites fled before their breads could rise—and it plays a starring role during Passover, when Jews honor the story of the exodus by avoiding leavened bread for eight days.

Most of us know matzah as the square, dry boards boxed and sold in stores. Commercial production ensures matzah is kosher for Passover, following all the rules about the harvesting and milling of the wheat as well as the baking (no more than 18 minutes can pass between mixing and baking, to prevent any possible fermentation or rising). Matzah can actually vary in shape and doesn't have to be hard—historically, and in some Mizrahi and Sephardi communities today, matzah is soft.

Dry and relatively flavorless matzah has spurred Jewish cooks to get creative. It's often ground into meal and used in coatings and fritters as well as dumplings (matzah balls!). It's coated in eggs and fried in matzah brei. Farfel, or crumbled matzah, is used in stuffings and kugels. There are Sephardi layered matzah pies and playful innovations like matzah "lasagna" (both included in this chapter).

As one of the best-known biblical foods, matzah serves as a powerful symbol of shared history, as well as a signature ingredient across Jewish culinary traditions.

Cheesy Stuffed Tomatoes

GLUTEN-FREE, KOSHER, VEGETARIAN / SERVES 6 TO 8
PREP TIME: 15 minutes / **COOK TIME:** 1 hour

Jewish cuisine overflows with stuffed vegetables (dolmas), whether they be grape or cabbage leaves or vegetables like bell peppers, zucchini, pumpkin, and tomatoes. Stuffed vegetables serve as both side and main dishes, and are especially enjoyed during Sukkot, where they symbolize abundance. This is a comforting cheesy-rice version of stuffed tomatoes.

Extra-virgin olive oil

1 medium sweet onion, finely chopped

1½ cups uncooked Arborio (short-grained) rice

3 cups water

½ teaspoon kosher salt

Freshly ground black pepper

⅓ cup ricotta

½ cup crumbled feta

⅛ teaspoon cayenne pepper

½ cup shredded Parmesan, plus more for topping

8 large, firm tomatoes, tops removed and insides hollowed out

---

1. Preheat the oven to 350°F and oil a 9-by-9-inch baking dish.

2. In a medium saucepan over medium heat, warm a layer of oil. Add the onion and rice and cook, stirring frequently, until onion softens slightly, 1 to 3 minutes. Add the water. Bring to a boil, cover, and reduce heat to low. Simmer without stirring for 15 minutes or until most liquid is absorbed.

3. Turn off the heat. Remove the lid and stir in the salt, pepper, ricotta, feta, cayenne, and ½ cup of Parmesan. Season to taste and cool slightly.

4. Fill the tomatoes with the rice mixture and place them in the baking dish. Sprinkle with Parmesan. Bake for about 30 minutes, until the tomatoes are soft and the topping is lightly browned. Serve warm.

VARIATION TIP: Garnish with a drizzle of pesto.

Lentil "Pizzas" (Lahmajin)

KOSHER, VEGETARIAN / SERVES 4 TO 6 (MAKES 4 [8-INCH] PIZZAS)
PREP TIME: 25 minutes, plus resting time / **COOK TIME:** 12 minutes

Lahmajin ("meat with dough") are popular flatbreads in Armenian, Turkish, and Syrian cuisine, as well as in Israel. They are usually topped with ground lamb or beef, but this Jewish vegetarian adaptation with a lentil topping tastes splendidly earthy and just as sensational. This recipe is adapted from Gil Marks's recipe in Olive Trees and Honey.

---

1 package store-bought pizza dough

1 cup brown lentils, cooked according to the package instructions

½ small onion, minced (about ⅓ cup)

3 tablespoons pomegranate molasses

3 tablespoons tomato paste

⅛ teaspoon crushed red pepper flakes

3 tablespoons extra-virgin olive oil, plus more for garnish

¾ teaspoon kosher salt, plus more for garnish

½ cup pine nuts (optional)

---

1. Preheat the oven to 500°F and line 2 large sheet pans with parchment paper.

2. Divide the pizza dough into 4 balls, cover, and let rest 15 minutes.

3. Mash the cooked lentils with a fork or potato masher. In a medium bowl, combine the lentils, onion, pomegranate molasses, tomato paste, crushed red pepper, olive oil, and kosher salt.

4. On a lightly floured surface, roll each dough ball into a roughly 8-inch round or square, about ⅛ inch thick. Transfer to the prepared sheet pans and top with the lentil filling and pine nuts, if using.

5. Bake 10 to 12 minutes or until edges are golden, rotating the pans halfway through. Serve warm, garnished with extra kosher salt and olive oil to taste.

Rustic Artichoke Tart

KOSHER, VEGETARIAN / SERVES 4 TO 6
PREP TIME: 20 minutes / **COOK TIME:** 35 minutes

Artichokes and vegetarian tarts and pies (pizzas) were both popular among Italy's Jews, and this recipe combines them in one satisfying dish. A rustic free-form crust makes it easy to bundle everything up.

---

2 tablespoons extra-virgin olive oil
1 large sweet onion, chopped
Kosher salt
Freshly ground black pepper
2 garlic cloves, minced
1 (12-ounce) bag frozen quartered artichoke hearts, thawed and coarsely chopped

1 (10-ounce) package pre-washed baby spinach or kale
Juice of ½ lemon
½ cup finely chopped flat-leaf parsley
¼ teaspoon ground nutmeg
2 eggs, lightly beaten
Store-bought pie dough, enough for 1 crust
½ cup grated Parmesan cheese (optional)

---

1. Preheat the oven to 350°F and line a sheet pan with parchment paper.

2. Warm the olive oil in a large nonstick skillet over medium-high heat. Add the onion, season lightly with salt and pepper, and cook until softened, stirring frequently, 3 to 5 minutes. Stir in the garlic and artichokes and cook for 2 to 3 more minutes, until lightly browned. Add the spinach or kale, cover, and cook without stirring until wilted, 3 to 5 minutes.

3. Stir in the lemon juice, parsley, nutmeg, and additional salt and pepper to taste. Cook 1 more minute. Let cool briefly and then fold in the eggs.

4. Place the pie crust on the sheet pan. Pile the filling in the center, leaving a 1½- to 2-inch border.

5. Fold the edges up to partially enclose the filling. Sprinkle the exposed filling with Parmesan, if using. Bake about 25 minutes, until crust is golden. Cool 10 minutes before serving.

Roasted Vegetable Moussaka

GLUTEN-FREE, KOSHER, VEGETARIAN / SERVES 6 TO 8
PREP TIME: 30 minutes / **COOK TIME:** 1 hour 45 minutes

In Greek cuisine, meat-filled eggplant moussaka often includes a top layer of dairy béchamel. Kosher versions of this layered eggplant casserole go either dairy-free or meat-free. This vegetarian adaptation gets its robust flavor from roasted eggplant and mushrooms with an easy labneh topping.

3½ to 4 pounds eggplant (4 medium eggplants), peeled and sliced into ½-inch rounds

Extra-virgin olive oil

Kosher salt

Freshly ground black pepper

1 pound mixed mushrooms, such as shiitake and cremini, chopped

1 large onion, finely chopped

2 garlic cloves, minced

1 teaspoon dried oregano

1 (28-ounce) can crushed tomatoes

¾ cup dry red wine

1 egg, plus 1 egg yolk

1 (16-ounce) container labneh (strained yogurt)

1 cup grated Parmesan, divided

½ teaspoon ground nutmeg

1. Preheat the oven to 400°F and line 3 sheet pans with nonstick aluminum foil.

2. Toss the eggplant with olive oil to coat and salt and pepper to taste directly on 2 sheet pans. Spread in a single layer and roast for 30 to 40 minutes or until lightly browned, turning once halfway through. Set aside.

3. On the third sheet pan, toss the mushrooms with oil to coat and salt and pepper to taste. Spread in a single layer and roast 30 to 40 minutes, stirring once, until lightly browned. Set aside.

4. Adjust the oven temperature to 350°F and oil a 9-by-13-inch baking dish.

5. Meanwhile, heat a layer of olive oil in a large saucepan over medium-high heat. Add the onion, season with salt and pepper, and cook until softened, stirring frequently, 3 to 5 minutes. Add the garlic and oregano and cook for 1 minute, stirring constantly. Stir in the tomatoes and red wine. Cover and simmer 10 minutes, then cook 5 minutes uncovered to thicken slightly.

6. In a medium bowl, lightly beat the egg and egg yolk. Stir in the labneh, ½ cup of Parmesan, nutmeg, ½ teaspoon of salt, and pepper to taste.

7. Layer a third of the eggplant and half of the mushrooms in the baking dish and top with a layer of tomato sauce. Repeat in the same order: eggplant, mushrooms, sauce. Finish with the last third of the eggplant, then cover completely with the labneh mixture. Sprinkle with the remaining Parmesan.

8. Bake the moussaka until the top is golden brown, about 30 minutes. Cool 15 minutes before serving.

VARIATION TIP: Substitute a traditional béchamel sauce for the labneh topping, if preferred.

Zucchini and Potato Fritada

GLUTEN-FREE, KOSHER, VEGETARIAN / SERVES 4 TO 6
PREP TIME: 30 minutes / **COOK TIME:** 50 minutes

A cousin to the Italian frittata, the Sephardi fritada employs favorite vegetables like leeks, spinach, zucchini, and tomatoes, along with mashed potatoes. Although traditionally prepared in a skillet, easier baked versions (also called quajado)—like this one—have become popular.

---

2 tablespoons unsalted butter at room temperature, or extra-virgin olive oil

3 medium zucchinis (2 pounds)

1 tablespoon kosher salt, plus more to taste

2 medium russet potatoes (1 pound), peeled and cut into chunks

7 eggs

6 scallions, thinly sliced, with some green parts

1½ cups crumbled feta

Freshly ground black pepper

Paprika or cayenne pepper, optional

---

1. Preheat the oven to 350°F and generously grease a 9-by-13-inch glass baking dish with butter or oil.

2. Shred the zucchini on the large holes of a box grater. Place it in a colander in the sink, toss with about 1 tablespoon kosher salt, and let drain about 30 minutes. Rinse and squeeze to dry.

3. While the zucchini drains, boil the potatoes covered in salted water until tender, about 20 minutes. Drain and mash with a potato masher.

4. In a large bowl, lightly beat the eggs. Stir in the zucchini, mashed potatoes, scallions, feta, and salt and pepper to taste.

5. Transfer to the baking dish and smooth the top. Sprinkle with paprika, if using. Bake until set and golden, about 30 minutes. Cool 15 minutes before serving.

STORAGE TIP: Leftovers can be refrigerated for up to 3 days or frozen for up to a month. Reheat in the microwave or in the oven at 350°F.

Lemon-Fennel Pasta Salad

KOSHER, VEGETARIAN / SERVES 4 TO 6
PREP TIME: 25 minutes, plus chilling time / **COOK TIME:** 10 minutes

Because of Shabbat prohibitions on cooking, Jews in Italy centuries ago may have been among the first to eat cold pasta dishes. These precursors to pasta salad were eaten with cold tomato or lemon sauces. In a modern take on that tradition, here's a pasta salad featuring the refreshing flavors of lemon and fennel, frequent ingredients in Italian-Jewish cooking.

---

16 ounces penne pasta

⅓ cup freshly squeezed lemon juice

1 tablespoon white wine vinegar

½ cup extra-virgin olive oil

½ teaspoon kosher salt

Freshly ground black pepper

¼ to ½ teaspoon crushed red pepper flakes, minced

1½ teaspoons dried oregano

1 fennel bulb, thinly sliced

1 rib of celery, thinly sliced

1 red bell pepper, thinly sliced into ½-inch strips

1 can white beans, such as cannellini, rinsed and drained

¼ cup chopped fresh basil leaves

---

1. Cook the pasta according to package instructions.

2. While the pasta cooks, make the dressing. In a medium bowl, whisk together the lemon juice, vinegar, olive oil, salt, pepper, red pepper flakes, and oregano.

3. Once cooked, drain the pasta and transfer it to a large bowl. Stir in the fennel, celery, bell pepper, beans, and basil. Toss with just enough dressing to coat, reserving the rest. Cover and chill at least 1 hour. Season to taste, adding dressing as needed. Serve cold or at room temperature.

VARIATION TIP: A sprinkle of lemon zest makes a flavorful garnish.

Chickpea Sambousak

KOSHER, VEGETARIAN / SERVES 4 TO 6 (MAKES 10 PASTRIES)
PREP TIME: 30 minutes / **COOK TIME:** 25 minutes

Handheld pastry turnovers are found throughout historical Sephardi and Mizrahi Jewish regions—consider bourekas, empanadas, and samosas. Perhaps one of the earliest of these—sambousak—comes from what is now Iraq, where chickpea fillings became a Jewish specialty. Originally deep-fried, the half-moon–shaped sambousak are now usually baked and make regular appearances for Hanukkah, Shavuot, and Purim meals.

---

1 tablespoon extra-virgin olive oil

1 medium onion, finely chopped

Kosher salt

Freshly ground black pepper

1 teaspoon ground cumin

½ teaspoon ground turmeric

1 (15.5-ounce) can chickpeas, drained and mashed

10 store-bought empanada wrappers

1 egg yolk, lightly beaten with 1 teaspoon cold water, or olive oil cooking spray

Sesame seeds for sprinkling

---

1. Preheat the oven to 375°F and line a large sheet pan with parchment paper.

2. Heat the olive oil in a medium nonstick skillet over medium-high heat. Add the onion and season lightly with salt and pepper. Cook, stirring frequently, for 3 to 5 minutes or until softened. Add the cumin and turmeric and cook for 1 minute, stirring constantly. Remove from the heat, stir in the chickpeas, and add salt and pepper to taste.

3. Lay the wrappers on a flat work surface. Spoon 2 tablespoons of filling into the center of each wrapper. Fold the wrappers over to make half-moons, pressing firmly and crimping the edges with a fork.

4. Transfer the sambousak to the sheet pan, brush with egg wash, and sprinkle with sesame seeds. Bake until golden, about 20 minutes. Serve warm or at room temperature.

Pea and Cheese Curry (Mattar Paneer) with Cauliflower

GLUTEN-FREE, KOSHER, VEGETARIAN / SERVES 4
PREP TIME: 25 minutes / **COOK TIME:** 20 minutes

According to food historian Claudia Roden, the popular North Indian dish mattar paneer was a dairy meal enjoyed by Jews of the Indian subcontinent. Cauliflower was also frequently used, so I've included it in this robustly flavored adaptation. Paneer cheese is traditional, but firm mozzarella works nicely, too. Serve with hot rice.

Extra-virgin olive oil

1 medium yellow onion, chopped

Kosher salt

Freshly ground black pepper

2 garlic cloves, minced

1½ teaspoons grated fresh ginger

1 teaspoon turmeric

1½ teaspoons garam masala

1 (28-ounce) can tomato puree or crushed tomatoes

2 teaspoons tomato paste

1 small head of cauliflower, cut into bite-size florets (about 3 cups)

1½ cups water

8 ounces frozen peas, about 1½ cups

8 ounces paneer or firm mozzarella, cut into ¾-inch cubes

---

1. Heat a layer of olive oil in a Dutch oven or other deep-sided pan over medium heat. Add the onion and season lightly with salt and pepper. Cook, stirring frequently, 3 to 5 minutes or until softened.

2. Add the garlic, ginger, turmeric, and garam masala and cook for 1 minute, stirring constantly. Add the tomato puree, tomato paste, cauliflower, and water. Bring to a boil, then cover, reduce the heat to low, and simmer for 12 minutes.

3. Add the frozen peas and cook for 2 additional minutes, then add the cheese and cook 2 to 3 more minutes to warm (but not melt) the cheese. Season to taste and serve with rice.

INGREDIENT TIP: Find garam marsala—a spice blend central to much Indian cooking—at most major supermarkets.

Falafel

FAMILY-FRIENDLY, KOSHER, VEGETARIAN / SERVES 4 TO 6 (MAKES 35 TO 40)
PREP TIME: 25 minutes, plus overnight soaking and chilling time / **COOK TIME:** 15 minutes

Falafel is an adored dish in Israel, and the love affair with these inexpensive protein-rich fritters goes back centuries in Middle Eastern cuisine. Enjoy hot falafel in warm Pita Bread (page 149) with chopped tomatoes and cucumbers, Zhug (page 63), pickles, or tahini sauce.

1½ cups dried chickpeas, soaked in cold water for 12 hours in the refrigerator (or 3 cups canned, drained)

½ medium yellow onion, chopped

3 garlic cloves

⅓ cup chopped fresh flat-leaf parsley or cilantro

1 teaspoon ground cumin

¼ teaspoon cayenne pepper

1 teaspoon kosher salt

Freshly ground black pepper

3 tablespoons all-purpose flour, plus more as needed

1½ teaspoons baking powder

Vegetable oil for frying

1. Drain the chickpeas.

2. In a food processor, combine the chickpeas, onion, garlic, parsley, cumin, cayenne pepper, salt, and black pepper to taste. Process (in batches if using a small processor) until the mixture is coarse, like very finely chopped nuts.

3. Transfer the mixture to a bowl and stir in the flour and baking powder, adding more flour as needed so small clumps will hold together. Chill for at least 1 hour.

4. Form the dough into 1-inch balls (keep them small to ensure even cooking), discarding any larger chunks of chickpeas that the processor missed.

 5. In a large deep-sided Dutch oven or other heavy pan on the stovetop, heat 1½ to 2 inches of oil to 325°F. Fry the falafel balls in batches, turning occasionally, until well browned (about 5 minutes). Drain on a plate lined with paper towels. Serve hot.

VARIATION TIP: For a quick tahini sauce, combine ¼ cup of tahini with 2 tablespoons of freshly squeezed lemon juice. Gradually stir in water to achieve a loose sauce consistency. Add ⅛ teaspoon kosher salt or more to taste, freshly ground black pepper to taste, a pinch of sugar, and paprika, hot paprika, or cumin to taste.

Sauerkraut with Fennel and Potatoes

GLUTEN-FREE, KOSHER, VEGETARIAN / SERVES 6 TO 8
PREP TIME: 20 minutes / **COOK TIME:** 1 hour 20 minutes

Ashkenazi Jews in Alsace, France, harbored a love of sauerkraut, shredded fermented cabbage that could be cooked overnight in Shabbat stews. Vegetables—like cabbage—that could be preserved with lacto-fermentation became customary in Ashkenazi cuisine throughout Europe. Sauerkraut was often cooked with cured meats, typical of Alsace cuisine, but this vegetarian version gets its heartiness from fennel and potatoes.

2 tablespoons extra-virgin olive oil

1 large sweet onion, finely chopped

1 cup finely chopped celery

2 medium fennel bulbs, halved, cored, and thinly sliced

Kosher salt

Freshly ground black pepper

2 pounds store-bought sauerkraut, drained

2 cups white wine, like Pinot Grigio

1 teaspoon caraway seeds

1 cup water

1 to 1½ pounds baby potatoes, unpeeled and halved (or quartered if large)

1. In a large Dutch oven or other heavy deep-sided pan, heat the oil over medium-high heat. Add the onion, celery, and fennel and season with salt and pepper. Cook for 7 to 10 minutes, or until just softened, stirring frequently.

2. Stir in the sauerkraut, white wine, caraway seeds, and water. Reduce the heat to low and simmer partially covered for 40 minutes, stirring occasionally.

3. Stir in the potatoes and add more water as needed. Continue cooking partially covered until the potatoes are tender, 20 to 30 minutes. Season to taste and serve hot.

Sephardi Spinach and Cheese Matzah Pie

KOSHER, VEGETARIAN / SERVES 2 TO 4
PREP TIME: 30 minutes / **COOK TIME:** 35 minutes

Sephardi cuisine features lots of savory pies, and come Passover, those pies become matzah pies (mina). Fillings include meat or vegetables and cheeses, and the seasonings vary among Iberian, Turkish, and Middle Eastern traditions. Here, a cheesy spinach filling with dill contrasts nicely with a crispy matzah top.

Extra-virgin olive oil

1 large yellow onion, finely chopped

Kosher salt

Freshly ground black pepper

1 (1-pound) bag frozen chopped spinach, thawed and excess liquid squeezed out

1 cup crumbled feta

1 cup grated Gruyère cheese

1 teaspoon dried dill

¼ teaspoon ground nutmeg

2 eggs, lightly beaten

2 to 4 matzah boards

1. Preheat the oven to 350°F and oil an 8-by-8-inch baking dish.

2. Warm a thin layer of oil in a large nonstick skillet over medium-high heat. Add the onion, season with salt and pepper, and cook 3 to 5 minutes or until softened, stirring frequently. Stir in the spinach and cook 1 minute, stirring constantly. Remove from heat and stir in feta, Gruyère, dill, nutmeg, and eggs.

3. Fill a wide bowl with warm water. Soak the matzah boards one at a time until soft, but not falling apart, 1 to 2 minutes. Remove, shake off excess water, and place a single layer on the bottom of the baking dish. Add the filling, then top with another layer of softened matzah. Brush the top with oil.

4. Bake uncovered until lightly browned, about 30 minutes. Cool 10 minutes before serving.

Matzah Lasagna, Italian-American Style

FAMILY-FRIENDLY, KOSHER, VEGETARIAN / SERVES 6 TO 8
PREP TIME: 30 minutes / **COOK TIME:** 1 hour, plus 15 minutes resting time

It doesn't matter whether you think of this dish as an Italian-American take on Sephardi mina (Passover pie) or a Passover take on a beloved Italian-American dish. Either way, matzah lasagna has become a crowd-pleasing Jewish family favorite in recent years, especially in the United States. For a shortcut, use 5½ cups of store-bought sauce.

FOR THE SAUCE

2 tablespoons extra-virgin olive oil

1 large onion, chopped

Kosher salt

Freshly ground black pepper

1½ teaspoons dried oregano

4 large garlic cloves, minced

½ teaspoon crushed red pepper flakes

3 (14.5-ounce) cans crushed tomatoes

FOR THE LASAGNA

2 pounds whole milk ricotta

2 eggs lightly beaten

⅓ cup chopped basil leaves

½ teaspoon kosher salt

Freshly ground black pepper

6 to 8 sheets store-bought matzah

16 ounces part-skim mozzarella, sliced and torn into bite-size pieces

¾ cup shredded Parmesan, for topping

TO MAKE THE SAUCE

1. In a large saucepan or Dutch oven over medium-high heat, warm the olive oil. Add the onion, season with salt and pepper, and cook 2 to 3 minutes or until softened, stirring frequently. Add the oregano, garlic, and red pepper flakes and cook for 1 minute, stirring constantly. Stir in the tomatoes, cover, and simmer for 15 minutes. Taste for seasoning.

TO MAKE THE LASAGNA

2. Preheat the oven to 375°F.

3. In a medium bowl, combine the ricotta, eggs, basil, ½ teaspoon kosher salt, and black pepper to taste.

4. Spread ½ cup of the sauce over the bottom of a 9-by-13-inch baking dish. Place matzah over the sauce in a single layer, breaking to fit as needed. Spread on half the ricotta mixture, half the mozzarella, and a thin layer of sauce.

5. Repeat, then top with a final layer of matzah. Cover completely with sauce, and sprinkle with Parmesan.

6. Cover with foil and bake for 30 minutes; then remove the foil and bake for 15 more minutes, until the top is bubbly and lightly browned. Cool 15 minutes before serving.

Lemon-Garlic Roast Chicken
Page 97

Chicken, Meat & Fish

TAKING IT SLOW

It was a uniquely Jewish culinary challenge: How does one have a hot meal on Saturday afternoon when Shabbat observance prohibits cooking for 24 hours after sundown on Friday? The answer has become a hallmark of Jewish cooking worldwide—the long-simmered, one-pot stew.

Two millennia ago, Jews in the Middle East turned a regional grain porridge into an overnight stew called harisa, adding meat and sometimes onions. Later on, Sephardi Jews in Spain added in beans, eggs, and more water. It became known as hamin (Hebrew for "hot") or adafina or dafina (Arabic for "buried"). Those stews went on to become the cholents of Ashkenazi Jews in France (possibly inspiring the French cassoulet) and Germany, which often used the only cuts of meat the Jews of the time could afford: brisket and short ribs. Slow-cooking suited the fatty, tough cuts perfectly and helped establish their enduring association with Jewish cuisine. The overnight bean-and-meat stew spread, morphing into versions with cumin in Morocco or garam masala in India.

Slow-cooking inspired more than just lasting dishes. In America, inventor Irving Nachumsohn, remembering his grandmother's tales of taking her cholent to the public bakery in Lithuania (since no one had private ovens), thought of a fix. He invented an electric appliance that allowed for slow simmering, and in 1940 the precursor to today's Crock-Pot was born.

Stews nowadays aren't usually cooked overnight, but the legacy of the technique lives on, featured prominently and deliciously in the Jewish culinary repertoire.

Lemon-Garlic Roast Chicken

GLUTEN-FREE, KOSHER / SERVES 4
PREP TIME: 15 minutes / **COOK TIME:** 1 hour, plus 20 minutes resting time

By way of its frequent and celebrated presence at Shabbat dinners starting in the twentieth century, roast chicken has become central to the Jewish culinary repertoire. Simple flavors like lemon, garlic, rosemary, and other herbs are all this dish needs to feel comforting but special, especially when drizzled with flavor-packed pan juices.

---

1 3½- to 4-pound whole chicken, patted dry
2 lemons, halved and seeded, divided
4 garlic cloves, smashed with a pinch of kosher salt

Kosher salt
Freshly ground black pepper
2 sprigs fresh rosemary
¼ cup extra-virgin olive oil

---

1. Preheat the oven to 425°F.

2. Rub the chicken all over with half of a lemon and the smashed garlic cloves. Season liberally with kosher salt and black pepper to taste. Place the rosemary sprigs, another lemon half, and any remaining garlic in the chicken's cavity. Truss the chicken if preferred, but it's not necessary.

3. Place the chicken breast-side up in an oven-safe skillet or roasting pan. Place the remaining lemon halves on either side of the chicken and drizzle with oil.

4. Roast until browned and cooked through, 40 to 60 minutes—the thickest part of the thigh should read 165°F.

5. Remove the pan from the oven and tent it with foil. Let it rest for 20 minutes. Drizzle the chicken with juices combined with chopped garlic pieces from the pan and serve warm.

VARIATION TIP: Chop rosemary, sage, or parsley and rub into the chicken skin before roasting.

Jewish-Italian Fried Chicken

FAMILY-FRIENDLY, KOSHER / SERVES 4 TO 6
PREP TIME: 15 minutes, plus 3 hours marinating time / **COOK TIME:** 20 minutes

Fried chicken? This might not seem like a Jewish dish at first glance, but it was widely prepared among Italy's Jewish community—especially for Hanukkah, when Jews eat foods fried in oil. Traditional preparations include a lemon marinade with warm spices, like cinnamon and nutmeg. To fry safely, use a deep-fry thermometer to monitor the temperature of the oil.

FOR THE MARINATED CHICKEN

2 tablespoons extra-virgin olive oil

¼ cup freshly squeezed lemon juice

½ teaspoon ground nutmeg

1 teaspoon garlic powder

3 teaspoons kosher salt

Freshly ground black pepper

1 whole chicken (about 3 pounds), cut into 10 pieces (by a butcher)

FOR FRYING

1 cup all-purpose flour

½ teaspoon garlic powder

½ teaspoon kosher salt

Freshly ground black pepper

Pinch of cayenne pepper

3 eggs, lightly beaten

Vegetable oil for frying (2 to 2½ quarts)

TO MAKE THE MARINADE

1. In a bowl or large resealable bag, combine the olive oil, lemon juice, nutmeg, garlic powder, salt, and black pepper. Add the chicken and stir or turn to coat.

2. Marinate in the refrigerator for 1 to 3 hours, stirring or turning a few times.

TO MAKE THE CHICKEN

3. In a wide, shallow bowl, whisk together the flour, garlic powder, salt, black pepper, and cayenne pepper. Dredge the chicken pieces first in the flour mixture, then in the eggs—the traditional method—and set aside on a plate.

4. In a large Dutch oven or other heavy deep-sided pan over medium-high heat, bring about 2½ inches of oil to 375°F.

5. Working in batches, slide the coated pieces into the oil. Adjust the burner continuously to keep the oil temperature around 325°F. Fry the chicken, turning occasionally, until golden and an instant-read thermometer inserted into the thickest part of each piece registers 165°F (10 to 15 minutes).

6. As they finish, transfer the fried chicken pieces to a paper towel–lined plate. Season to taste and serve hot.

SUBSTITUTION TIP: If you prefer dark meat (which tends to stay moister during frying), substitute bone-in, skin-in chicken thighs and drumsticks for the whole chicken.

Chicken with Apples and Dried Cherries

FAMILY-FRIENDLY, GLUTEN-FREE, KOSHER / SERVES 4 TO 6
PREP TIME: 10 minutes, plus 30 minutes marinating time / **COOK TIME:** 30 minutes

Flavor contrasts are central to Sephardi cooking, with chicken cooked with fruit embodying that well. In my modern and easy sheet-pan preparation, cherry preserves give the chicken beautiful color and flavor. The apples turn silky soft and the sour cherries develop an almost candy-like quality during broiling.

2½ to 3 pounds bone-in, skin-on chicken thighs, patted dry and fat trimmed

1 cup dried sweetened sour cherries

¾ cup black cherry preserves

2 tablespoons balsamic vinegar

3½ tablespoons extra-virgin olive oil, divided

1½ teaspoons kosher salt, divided

¼ teaspoon cayenne pepper

Freshly ground black pepper

2 medium tart apples, such as Granny Smith, cored and sliced into 8 wedges each

1 large sweet onion, halved and thinly sliced

---

1. In a bowl or large resealable bag, combine the chicken, cherries, preserves, vinegar, 2 tablespoons of olive oil, 1 teaspoon kosher salt, cayenne pepper, and black pepper to taste. Marinate at room temperature for 30 minutes, turning several times.

2. Preheat the oven to 425°F and line a large rimmed sheet pan with aluminum foil.

3. On the sheet pan, toss the apples and onion with the remaining 1½ tablespoons olive oil, ½ teaspoon salt, and pepper to taste.

4. Add the cherries and chicken (skin-side up) to the sheet pan in a single layer, ensuring a few cherries rest on top.

5. Bake for 25 to 30 minutes or until cooked through. (An instant-read thermometer inserted in the thickest part of the thigh should read 165°F.)

6. Turn the broiler to high and adjust rack to be nearest to broiler. Broil until just crisped, 2 to 4 minutes. Let rest for 5 minutes before serving. Season to taste.

✳ Chicken Sofrito

GLUTEN-FREE, KOSHER / SERVES 4
PREP TIME: 15 minutes / **COOK TIME:** 1 hour

Sofrito sometimes refers to an aromatic sauce, but for Sephardi Jews, it refers to a prized method of slow-cooking chicken or other meat in seasoned broth. This simple technique produces tender, juicy, flavorful results, making it a longtime favorite for Shabbat dinners. Serve with rice, bread, or crispy roasted potatoes.

Extra-virgin olive oil
1 3½- to 4-pound whole chicken, quartered and patted dry
1 medium onion, halved and sliced
Kosher salt
Freshly ground black pepper

1 teaspoon ground turmeric
½ teaspoon ground cardamom
½ cup chicken broth or water
2 tablespoons freshly squeezed lemon juice

---

1. Heat a layer of oil in a large Dutch oven or deep-sided pan over medium-high heat. Working in batches if needed, sear the chicken pieces, skin-side down, about 5 minutes or until lightly browned. Transfer the chicken to a plate and reduce the heat to medium.

2. Add the onion to the pan. Season with salt and pepper and cook for 3 to 5 minutes or until softened, stirring frequently.

3. Return the chicken to the pan with the onion, this time skin-side up, and sprinkle with turmeric, cardamom, and salt and pepper to taste. Add the broth and lemon juice.

4. Reduce the heat to low, cover the pan, and cook for 1 hour, adding broth as needed if the pan seems dry, until chicken is the cooked through. (The interior temperature should be 165°F on an instant-read thermometer inserted into the thickest part of the chicken pieces.)

Doro Wot (Ethiopian Spicy Chicken)

GLUTEN-FREE, KOSHER / SERVES 6 TO 8
PREP TIME: 15 minutes / **COOK TIME:** 1 hour

The heat's on in Ethiopia's national dish, wot, a stew traditionally cooked in a clay pot seasoned liberally with the chile-based spice blend berbere. Ethiopian Jews cooked versions of this fiery, fragrant dish for Sabbath dinner, substituting oil for the typical ghee. Serve with rice or bread.

---

2 tablespoons extra-virgin olive oil

2 large yellow onions, finely chopped

Kosher salt

Freshly ground black pepper

4 garlic cloves, minced

1 teaspoon minced fresh ginger

2 tablespoons berbere

1 4-pound chicken, cut into 8 or 10 pieces (by a butcher)

1 (6-ounce) can tomato paste

1 cup chicken broth or water

---

1. Heat the olive oil in a large Dutch oven or other deep-sided pan over medium heat. Add the onion, season with salt and pepper, and cook, stirring frequently, for 3 to 5 minutes or until softened.

2. Add the garlic, ginger, and berbere and cook for 1 minute, stirring constantly.

3. Adjust the heat to medium-high. Add the chicken and lightly sear both sides, about 3 minutes. Combine the tomato paste and broth and stir into the pan.

4. Cover and reduce the heat to low. Simmer, stirring occasionally, about 30 minutes. Uncover and cook 20 to 30 more minutes, until the sauce thickens and the chicken is tender and cooked through. (An instant-read thermometer inserted in the thickest part of the thigh should read 165°F.) Let rest, loosely covered, for a few minutes before serving.

INGREDIENT TIP: Find berbere at specialty stores or buy it online.

Brisket with Red Wine and Tomatoes

GLUTEN-FREE, KOSHER / SERVES 4 TO 6
PREP TIME: 45 minutes / **COOK TIME:** about 5 hours

Brisket, once considered an undesirable, tough cut of beef, was historically what poor Ashkenazi Eastern European Jews could afford. Cooking it low and slow made it tender and flavorful, and soon brisket became a base for cholents and tzimmes and a frequent holiday centerpiece. Make this robust version ahead. Allowing it to cool overnight makes it easier to trim the fat and slice it; plus, rewarming the brisket brings out its best flavor.

1 5-pound brisket, ideally with about a ¼-inch layer of fat

Kosher salt

Freshly ground black pepper

2 large yellow onions, halved and sliced

3 garlic cloves, halved

1 (28-ounce) can whole peeled tomatoes with juices

1 sprig fresh rosemary, plus additional for optional garnish

1½ cups dry red wine

½ cup beef stock or broth

1 tablespoon tomato paste

1. Preheat the oven to 325°F.

2. In a large skillet over high heat, brown the brisket on both sides, about 12 minutes. Season generously with salt and pepper to taste.

3. Place the onion, garlic, tomatoes, and rosemary sprig in a large roasting pan. Place the brisket on top, fat-side up. Pour the red wine, stock, and tomato paste on top. Cover with aluminum foil.

4. Roast for 3½ to 5 hours, or until the meat is fork-tender, basting a few times.

5. Transfer the meat to a dish, cover with a few spoonfuls of the cooking liquid (reserving the rest), and cool slightly. Cover and refrigerate overnight.

6. Strain and set the cooking liquids aside, reserving the solids. Cover and refrigerate the sauce and vegetables separately overnight.

7. The next day, skim most of the fat from the sauce, stirring in the rest. Trim the fatty layer from the brisket and slice the meat against the grain. Place the slices in a baking dish and spoon a little more sauce over the top. Cover with foil and reheat at 350°F until hot, 30 to 40 minutes.

8. Meanwhile, in a medium saucepan over medium-high heat, bring the remaining sauce to a boil. Cook for 10 to 15 minutes until reduced by about half.

9. Coarsely chop about 1 cup of the reserved garlic, onion, and tomatoes, and stir into the sauce to warm.

10. Transfer the brisket to a platter and arrange the chopped vegetables and sauce around it, reserving the rest of the sauce to pass around the table.

11. Garnish with chopped rosemary (if using), and serve warm.

INGREDIENT TIP: Give yourself leeway when making brisket, because cooking time will vary with the thickness and fattiness of the meat. Thinner cuts take around 3½ hours, but thicker, fattier cuts can take 5 hours or longer.

Meatballs in Tomato Sauce

FAMILY-FRIENDLY, KOSHER / SERVES 4 (MAKES 22 TO 26 MEATBALLS)
PREP TIME: 30 minutes / **COOK TIME:** 50 minutes

Meatballs (albondigas) have been a part of Jewish cuisine dating back centuries, when they were cooked by Sephardi Jews who adopted them from Spain's Muslim rulers. Meatballs became regulars on Shabbat and holiday tables, often made with lamb and typically served plain or with vinegar or lemon sauces until tomatoes became widely available. Here, cinnamon reflects the Middle Eastern heritage and adds warmth to the sauce. Serve traditional style, over rice.

FOR THE MEATBALLS

2 slices white bread, crusts removed

1 pound ground beef or lamb

1 egg, lightly beaten

½ medium onion, minced

½ teaspoon kosher salt

Freshly ground black pepper

¼ cup finely chopped fresh parsley

2 tablespoons extra-virgin olive oil

FOR THE SAUCE

1 medium onion, finely chopped

Kosher salt

Freshly ground black pepper

2 garlic cloves, minced

¼ teaspoon cinnamon

1 (28-ounce) can crushed tomatoes

2 tablespoons chopped flat-leaf parsley

MAKE THE MEATBALLS

1. Soak the white bread in water and then squeeze it to remove excess. (It should still be moist.)

2. In a large bowl, combine the meat, bread, egg, onion, salt, pepper, and parsley. Form into 1½-inch balls.

3. In a large Dutch oven over medium-high heat, warm the oil. Add the meatballs in a single layer, working in batches if needed. Fry until mostly browned, turning once or twice, 8 to 10 minutes. Transfer to a plate.

MAKE THE SAUCE

4. Add the onions to the still-hot pan, season with salt and pepper, and cook for 3 to 5 minutes or until softened, stirring frequently. Add the garlic and cinnamon and cook for 1 minute, stirring constantly.

5. Stir in the tomatoes and parsley, then the reserved meatballs. Partially cover, reduce the heat, and simmer for about 30 minutes. Serve hot.

> **VARIATION TIP:** If not observing kosher rules, add ¼ cup grated Parmesan cheese to the meatballs for flavor and tenderness.

Goulash (Hungarian Paprika Beef Stew)

GLUTEN-FREE, KOSHER / SERVES 4
PREP TIME: 20 minutes / **COOK TIME:** 3 hours

Paprika was introduced to Hungary in the late sixteenth century—and when combined with stew, a match was made in gastronomical heaven. Goulash has become one of Hungary's most famous dishes and was prepared by Hungarian Jews for Shabbat and other special occasions. It's most flavorful made a day ahead and gently reheated. Serve with potatoes or wide egg noodles.

2 tablespoons extra-virgin olive oil

2 to 3 large yellow onions, halved and thinly sliced

Kosher salt

Freshly ground black pepper

4 garlic cloves, minced

3 tablespoons paprika

½ teaspoon hot paprika or cayenne pepper

2 tablespoons tomato paste

2 pounds boneless beef chuck stew meat (1½-inch cubes)

2 cups beef broth

1. Warm the oil in a large Dutch oven over medium-low heat. Add the onion, season with salt and pepper, and turn to coat. Cover and cook for 10 minutes.

2. Uncover, stir, and reduce heat to low. Continue cooking about 10 minutes, until golden and very soft.

3. Add the garlic, paprika, hot paprika or cayenne pepper, and tomato paste and cook for 1 minute, stirring constantly. Add the beef and season with salt and pepper. Cook for 2 minutes, stirring occasionally.

4. Stir in the broth and bring to a boil; then cover and reduce the heat to simmer until tender, about 3 hours. Season to taste and serve hot.

Adafina (Short Rib Shabbat Stew)

GLUTEN-FREE, KOSHER / SERVES 6 TO 8
PREP TIME: 30 minutes / **COOK TIME:** 12 hours

Adafina (also known as dafina or d'fina) is a slow-cooked Shabbat stew with origins in North Africa. Its basic building blocks include beans, meat, onions, potatoes, garlic, cumin, and whole eggs—other ingredients and spices vary by region and even by family. The traditional cut of beef is often flanken (short ribs cut across the bone), but boneless short ribs are easier to find and work well for this slow-cooker preparation.

2 (15.5 ounce) cans chickpeas, drained and rinsed

2 large yellow onions, coarsely chopped

6 garlic cloves, smashed

15 to 18 baby (two-bite size) Yukon Gold potatoes, unpeeled

3 pounds boneless beef short ribs, cut into chunks

8 eggs

4 cups beef broth or water

1 teaspoon kosher salt

Freshly ground black pepper

1 teaspoon ground turmeric

1 teaspoon ground cumin

½ teaspoon ground allspice

1. In a large slow cooker, combine the chickpeas, onions, garlic, potatoes, and beef. Nestle the eggs (still in their shells) on top.

2. In a medium bowl, whisk together the broth, salt, pepper, turmeric, cumin, and allspice and add to the slow cooker.

3. Cover and cook on the high setting for 1 hour, then on the low setting for 10 to 11 hours, or until meat is tender.

4. Just before serving, skim any fat from the surface. Remove and peel the eggs and return them to the stew. Season to taste and serve hot.

VARIATION TIP: If you don't have a slow cooker, simmer the stew on the stovetop for 3 to 4 hours, until the meat is tender.

✳ Turkey-Stuffed Cabbage

GLUTEN-FREE, KOSHER / SERVES 4 TO 6 (MAKES ABOUT 12 ROLLS)
PREP TIME: 40 minutes, plus resting time / **COOK TIME:** 2 hours

You've got to love a dish with the Yiddish name "galooptchy." And indeed, galooptchy—stuffed cabbage leaves in rich tomato sauce—are beloved in Ashkenazi cooking. This version gets its tenderness from ground turkey (which holds moisture better than the usual ground beef) and extra flavor from garlic powder and fennel seeds. Freezing the cabbage overnight softens the leaves for easy wrapping.

---

1 large head green cabbage

2 (15-ounce) cans tomato sauce

1½ teaspoons dried basil

2 tablespoons light brown sugar

1½ teaspoons kosher salt, divided

Freshly ground black pepper

1 egg

1 pound ground turkey (or ground beef chuck)

1 medium yellow onion, finely chopped

1½ teaspoons garlic powder

1 teaspoon fennel seeds

½ cup uncooked long-grain white rice

1 tablespoon extra-virgin olive oil

---

1. Remove one outer layer of cabbage leaves; then rinse and core the cabbage. Wrap and freeze overnight. About three hours before cooking, defrost the cabbage at room temperature.

2. Preheat the oven to 375°F.

3. In a medium bowl, combine the tomato sauce, basil, sugar, ½ teaspoon of the kosher salt, and pepper to taste. Spread a thin layer of this sauce in a 9-by-13-inch baking dish.

4. In a large bowl, lightly beat the egg. Stir in the turkey, onion, remaining 1 teaspoon of kosher salt, additional pepper to taste, garlic powder, fennel seeds, rice, olive oil, and 1 tablespoon of the tomato sauce mixture.

5. Peel off 12 large cabbage leaves.

6. Place about 3 tablespoons of filling on each leaf. Fold the stem end over the filling, fold in the sides, and then roll up like a burrito. Tightly pack the wraps, seam-side down, in the baking dish. Top with sauce. Cover and bake until the cabbage is tender and cuts easily, about 2 hours. Serve hot.

MAKE AHEAD TIP: The stuffed cabbage can be cooked 1 day ahead and covered and chilled. Reheat covered in a 350°F oven until hot, about 45 minutes.

Sephardi-Style Roast Lamb Shoulder

GLUTEN-FREE / SERVES 8 TO 10
PREP TIME: 10 minutes / **COOK TIME:** 4 hours

For many Sephardi Jews, roasted lamb shoulder is a festive dish for Passover and other holidays. The fatty cut of meat takes well to slow-roasting, and the nestled-in garlic slivers add great flavor.

---

1 4- to 5-pound boneless lamb
   shoulder roast
6 garlic cloves, slivered
1 sprig fresh rosemary
Extra-virgin olive oil

Kosher salt
Freshly ground black pepper
1 large onion, halved and sliced
1 cup chicken stock

---

1. Preheat the oven to 400°F.

2. Place lamb, fat-side up, on a rack in a large roasting pan. Cut evenly spaced slits on surface and insert garlic slivers. Tuck rosemary into the center of roast. Rub all over with oil to coat and season generously with salt and pepper. Add the onion to the pan and pour the stock into the bottom.

3. Place in the oven and immediately turn heat to 325°F. Roast for 2½ to 4 hours, to desired degree of doneness.

4. Let stand for 15 minutes before carving.

KOSHER TIP: Some Jewish communities avoid eating lamb or any roasted meats for the Passover Seder meal. Check with your trusted authority.

Poached Salmon with Lemon-Dill Sauce

GLUTEN-FREE, KOSHER / SERVES 4
PREP TIME: 10 minutes / **COOK TIME:** 10 minutes, plus chilling time

In Jewish tradition, fish symbolizes abundance and prosperity, so fish dishes are welcome at many occasions. Poached fish, which can be served warm or cold, has been perennially perfect for Shabbat, and Greek and Turkish Jews also served it to break the fast on Yom Kippur. This easy make-ahead version is modeled on a French white-wine poached salmon once popular among Jewish communities in Russia.

4 salmon fillets (about 2 pounds), 1 inch thick

2 cups dry white wine

3 teaspoons kosher salt, plus more to taste

2 bay leaves

½ cup sour cream

¼ cup freshly squeezed lemon juice

2 tablespoons chopped fresh dill

Freshly ground black pepper

 1. Place the salmon skin-side down in a large, wide pan. Add the wine, 3 teaspoons of kosher salt, and bay leaves. Add cold water to cover the fish.

2. Cover with a lid and bring to a boil, then turn off the heat and let stand covered until just cooked through, 8 to 10 minutes—the fish should flake easily. Carefully remove it to a platter.

3. Meanwhile, make the sauce. In a small bowl, combine the sour cream, lemon juice, dill, and salt and pepper to taste.

4. Keep the salmon and sauce covered and refrigerated separately until serving time. Serve the salmon chilled with lemon-dill sauce.

North African–Style Spicy Fish

GLUTEN-FREE, KOSHER / SERVES 4
PREP TIME: 10 minutes, plus resting time / **COOK TIME:** 12 minutes, plus 10 minutes cooling time

Jewish communities across North Africa—in Algeria, Libya, Morocco, and Tunisia—had regionally influenced variations of white fish poached in a spicy red sauce. Versions of this dish were served at Shabbat dinners, and today it's enjoyed across Israel. This boldly flavored rendition comes together easily and can be an appetizer or main dish. Serve with rice or bread.

Extra-virgin olive oil

8 garlic cloves, minced

2 teaspoons minced fresh red chiles or
  1 to 2 teaspoons crushed red pepper
  flakes, minced

2 teaspoons paprika

¼ cup freshly squeezed lemon juice

3 tablespoons tomato paste

Kosher salt

Freshly ground black pepper

¾ cup water

4 firm white fish fillets, such as
  halibut or cod

Chopped cilantro or parsley for garnish,
  optional

1. In a deep-sided pot or skillet over medium heat, warm a thin layer of oil. Add the garlic, chiles, and paprika and cook for 1 minute, stirring constantly.

2. Stir in the lemon juice, tomato paste, and salt and pepper to taste. Add the water and bring to a boil.

3. Gently add the fish, turn to coat, and cover. Reduce the heat to low and simmer until the fish is opaque and flakes easily with a fork, about 10 minutes. Remove from the heat, uncover, and let cool 10 minutes. Serve sprinkled with cilantro, if using.

VARIATION TIP: For a thicker sauce, remove the fish when done and boil the sauce for a few minutes to reduce.

Fried Fish with "Old Bay" Mayo

KOSHER / SERVES 4 TO 6
PREP TIME: 20 minutes, plus resting time / **COOK TIME:** 20 minutes

Long before fish and chips became identified with the British Isles, Sephardi Jews from around the Mediterranean fried battered fish in oil. After the Spanish expulsion in 1492, the Portuguese Jews who settled in Holland and England helped introduce and popularize the dish. My recipe is accompanied by a mayonnaise dip featuring Old Bay seasoning, a spice blend invented by a German-Jewish immigrant in Baltimore in 1939.

---

1 cup mayonnaise

2 teaspoons Old Bay seasoning

2½ cups all-purpose flour

½ cup cornstarch

2 teaspoons kosher salt, plus more to taste

Freshly ground black pepper

2 cups just-opened seltzer water

Olive or vegetable oil for frying

2 pounds ½- to 1-inch thick cod or halibut fillets, rinsed, patted dry, and cut into pieces (ideally about 1½ to 2 inches wide)

---

1. To make the dip: in a small bowl, combine the mayonnaise and Old Bay seasoning. Refrigerate until ready to serve.

2. To make the batter: In a medium bowl, whisk together the flour, cornstarch, salt, and pepper. Fold in the seltzer. Set aside at room temperature for 15 minutes.

3. In a large Dutch oven over medium-high heat, heat 2 inches of oil to 375°F.

4. Season the fish fillets with salt and pepper to taste. Working in batches, coat the fish in batter, then gently slide it into the oil to minimize splattering. Fry until golden brown, 4 to 8 minutes.

5. Remove to a paper towel–lined plate. Serve immediately with Old Bay mayo.

Wine-Poached Gefilte Fish

KOSHER / SERVES 12 TO 14 (MAKES 14 TO 16 PATTIES)
PREP TIME: 30 minutes / **COOK TIME:** 25 minutes

For many Eastern European Jews, it wouldn't be Rosh Hashanah or Passover without gefilte fish, an Old World delicacy. Yes, you can get it in a jar, but if you're a fan of this iconic appetizer, it's worth trying a homemade version. In this updated approach, the patties come out delicately tender with flavor brightened by white wine, parsley, and lemon. Serve with Beet Horseradish (page 60).

FOR THE BROTH

1 bottle dry white wine

8 cups water

3 bay leaves

2 tablespoons dried minced onions

2 teaspoons kosher salt

Freshly ground black pepper

FOR THE GEFILTE FISH

2 pounds skinned mild white fish fillets, such as a mix of halibut and cod, patted dry and cut into large chunks

1 large yellow onion, quartered

1 large carrot, cut into large chunks

2 large eggs, lightly beaten

1 tablespoon extra-virgin olive oil

¼ cup finely chopped flat-leaf parsley

½ teaspoon freshly squeezed lemon juice

¼ cup matzah meal, plus more as needed

1½ teaspoons kosher salt, plus more to taste

Freshly ground black pepper

TO MAKE THE BROTH

1. In a large wide pot, combine the wine, water, bay leaves, dried onions, salt, and a generous amount of black pepper to taste. Bring to a simmer.

TO MAKE THE GEFILTE FISH PATTIES

2. In a food processor, pulse the fish for a few seconds, until finely chopped but not pureed. Transfer to a mixing bowl.

3. Process the onion and carrot until nearly smooth and add to the fish, stirring to incorporate. Add the eggs, olive oil, parsley, lemon juice, matzah meal, salt, and pepper to taste. Stir to mix well.

4. Use your hands to form oval patties, about 2 by 3 inches and ½- to ¾-inch thick.

5. Slide the patties into the broth. Cover and simmer 20 to 25 minutes, or until cooked through. (The internal temperature on an instant-read thermometer should read 160°F.)

6. Remove from the heat and let cool in the broth for 15 minutes. Transfer the gefilte fish patties to a plate. Serve warm, at room temperature, or chilled.

Israeli Couscous with Tomato and Onion
Page 128

Chapter 7

Noodles, Grains & Beans

RICE: FIVE THOUSAND YEARS STRONG

Rice seems so commonplace that we tend to overlook its importance in Jewish culinary history. But most Sephardi and Mizrahi meals would not be complete without rice. This venerable grain has been cultivated in China and India for at least 5,000 years and spread to Persia more than 2,000 years ago, where it became a star ingredient.

Beginning around the ninth century CE, Arab conquerors brought rice from Persia to Spain, Sicily, North Africa, and other parts of Asia, where it was embraced by Jews across regions. Since rice doesn't grow well in most of Europe (excluding the southernmost regions, like Italy and Spain), it appears relatively infrequently in Ashkenazi cooking.

After their expulsion from Spain and southern Italy, Jews brought rice dishes to northern Italy, where risottos became signatures of Venetian cuisine. It's also hypothesized that Jewish saffron risotto, often cooked for Shabbat, inspired the famous dish risotto alla Milanese.

Today, rice remains one of most cultivated grains in the world. Whether prepared on its own (like in tahdig, where it develops a crispy bottom crust), stuffed in vegetables, served alongside a main dish (like a stew), or turned into a dessert, this ancient grain remains central.

Sweet Cheese Noodle Kugel

FAMILY-FRIENDLY, KOSHER, VEGETARIAN / SERVES 8 TO 10
PREP TIME: 15 minutes / **COOK TIME:** 40 minutes, plus 15 minutes resting time

For many Ashkenazi Jews, noodle kugels, whether sweet or savory, represent pure comfort in a baking dish. Somewhere between a quiche and a casserole, these baked puddings are all-stars, gracing Shabbat tables, holidays, and life-cycle events. My nicely sweet, richly custardy rendition can be a side dish or dessert.

---

4 tablespoons butter, melted, plus more for coating the dish

12 ounces wide egg noodles

8 ounces cream cheese, room temperature

⅓ cup light brown sugar

2 cups sour cream

8 ounces small-curd cottage cheese

6 eggs

1 teaspoon vanilla extract

½ teaspoon kosher salt

½ teaspoon ground cinnamon, plus more for topping

---

1. Preheat the oven to 350°F. Butter a 9-by-13-inch baking dish and set aside.

2. Cook egg noodles in salted water according to the package directions, then drain and set aside.

3. Meanwhile, in a very large bowl, combine the cream cheese and light brown sugar until smooth. Using a whisk or hand mixer, blend in the sour cream, cottage cheese, eggs, melted butter, vanilla extract, salt, and cinnamon. Fold in the noodles.

4. Transfer the mixture to the baking dish and smooth the top. Sprinkle with ground cinnamon. Bake until set and the top is lightly browned, about 30 minutes. Cool 15 minutes before serving. Serve warm or at room temperature.

VARIATION TIP: For extra sweetness and crunch, sprinkle with crushed graham crackers or cornflakes before baking.

Savory Noodle Kugel

KOSHER, VEGETARIAN / SERVES 6 TO 8
PREP TIME: 15 minutes / **COOK TIME:** 35 minutes, plus 5 minutes resting time

The earliest versions of kugels, which originated among German Ashkenazi Jews, were likely savory puddings of starch, fat, and eggs steamed alongside overnight Sabbath stews. Their appeal and versatility endures to this day. Here, a crunchy top, thick noodles, and peppery kick distinguish this savory nondairy version.

4 tablespoons extra-virgin olive oil, divided

8 ounces pappardelle pasta, broken roughly in half

1 medium yellow onion, finely chopped

1 teaspoon kosher salt, plus more to taste

½ teaspoon freshly ground black pepper, plus more to taste

3 garlic cloves, minced

¼ to ½ teaspoon crushed red pepper flakes

6 eggs

1. Preheat the oven to 350°F. Grease the bottom and sides of a 9-by-9-inch baking dish with 2 tablespoons of olive oil and set aside.

2. Cook the pasta according to package instructions. Drain and set aside.

3. Warm 1 tablespoon of olive oil in a medium nonstick skillet over medium-high heat. Add the onion, season with salt and pepper to taste, and cook 3 to 5 minutes or until softened, stirring frequently. Add the garlic and red pepper flakes and cook for 1 minute, stirring constantly. Set aside.

4. In a large bowl, lightly beat the eggs, then fold in the noodles, onion mixture, remaining 1 tablespoon of olive oil, 1 teaspoon salt, and ½ teaspoon pepper, plus more to taste. Transfer to the baking dish and spread in an even layer.

5. Bake until golden and slightly crispy, about 30 minutes. Let rest for about 5 minutes, then serve warm or at room temperature.

VARIATION TIP: For extra crunch, sprinkle panko breadcrumbs on top before baking.

Kreplach

FAMILY-FRIENDLY, KOSHER / MAKES ABOUT 25
PREP TIME: 25 minutes, plus 10 minutes chilling time / **COOK TIME:** 15 minutes

Food historians believe Chinese wontons inspired these Jewish stuffed pasta dumplings, which are also cousins of Polish pierogi and Italian tortellini. Eastern European Jews made kreplach to repurpose left-over meat as a filling (and cheese versions were enjoyed especially for Shavuot). They are best made with pasta dough, but wonton wrappers are faster and just as crowd-pleasing, especially when double-layered and fried (though they can also be served in hot soup). This recipe offers the option for either a meat or a cheese filling.

FOR A MEAT FILLING
1½ to 2 cups finely chopped Brisket with Red Wine and Tomatoes (page 104) or Lemon-Garlic Roast Chicken (page 97)

FOR A CHEESE FILLING
1½ cups ricotta
1 cup grated Parmesan
½ teaspoon nutmeg

Kosher salt
Freshly ground black pepper

FOR THE DUMPLINGS
1 (12-ounce) package wonton wrappers
Extra-virgin olive oil
Crushed red pepper flakes (optional)
Chopped fresh chives for garnish (optional)

TO MAKE THE FILLING

1. Prepare the meat filling of your choice. Alternately, prepare the cheese filling in a medium bowl by combining the ricotta, Parmesan, nutmeg, and salt and pepper to taste.

CONTINUED

TO MAKE THE DUMPLINGS

2. Create double wrappers by moistening one wrapper with water and firmly pressing another wrapper on top.

3. Place 2 teaspoons of filling on a double wrapper, just off-center. Dip your finger in water and moisten the outer border of the wrapper. Fold the wrapper over the filling into a triangle, sealing the edges firmly. Repeat with the remaining wrappers and filling.

4. Transfer the kreplach to a sheet pan lined with wax paper and freeze for 10 minutes.

5. Meanwhile, bring a large pot of salted water to boil. Working in batches if needed, boil the kreplach, stirring frequently until al dente, 2 to 4 minutes.

6. Remove kreplach with a slotted spoon.

7. To fry, heat a layer of olive oil in a large nonstick skillet over medium heat. Working in batches, add kreplach in a single layer, season with salt and pepper, and fry 4 to 6 minutes, until browned and crisp on both sides. Serve hot, garnished with crushed red pepper and fresh chives, if using.

MAKE AHEAD TIP: Freeze boiled kreplach for up to 1 month. Fry directly from the freezer, covered over low heat for 2 minutes, then uncovered over medium heat until browned, 1 to 2 more minutes.

Kasha Varnishkes

KOSHER, VEGETARIAN / SERVES 8 TO 10
PREP TIME: 15 minutes / **COOK TIME:** 30 minutes

This beloved dish of Ukrainian origin might seem humble, but it pushes all the comfort food buttons—sweet caramelized onions, nutty toasted buckwheat kernels, and tender and filling pasta. Modern touches of tricolor pasta, red onion, and red pepper flakes add color and flavor.

---

12 ounces tricolor farfalle pasta

Extra-virgin olive oil

1 large sweet onion, chopped

1 large red onion, chopped

Kosher salt

Freshly ground black pepper

Pinch red pepper flakes, optional

2 cups water

1 cup kasha (roasted buckwheat)

1 egg, lightly beaten

---

1. Cook the pasta al dente according to package instructions. Drain, transfer to a large serving bowl, and toss lightly with oil to coat. Set aside.

2. Heat a layer of oil in a large nonstick skillet over medium-high heat. Add the onions, season with salt and pepper, and stir. Cover, reduce heat to low, and cook for 10 minutes.

3. Uncover, stir again, and cook 10 more minutes, or until softened and deep golden brown, stirring occasionally. Stir in the red pepper flakes, if using.

4. Meanwhile, in a small pan, bring the water to boil.

5. While the water heats, combine the kasha and egg in a medium saucepan over medium heat. Cook 2 to 3 minutes or until the kernels are dry and toasted, stirring constantly. Season with salt and pepper; then stir in the boiling water. Cover, reduce the heat to low, and simmer about 8 minutes, until the liquid is absorbed.

6. Add the kasha mixture to the pasta and stir to incorporate. Toss in the onions with a little more oil, if desired. Season to taste and serve warm.

INGREDIENT TIP: Be sure to buy kasha (roasted buckwheat) and not raw buckwheat groats, which are chewier and less flavorful.

Bulgur and Beef "Kibbeh" Pie

KOSHER / SERVES 6 TO 8
PREP TIME: 30 minutes / **COOK TIME:** 45 minutes, plus 15 minutes cooling time

A national dish of Syria and Lebanon, now popular in Israel, kibbeh is a deep-fried torpedo-shaped croquette made with ground meat and surrounded by a seasoned bulgur shell. Since shaping and frying the kibbeh takes time and skill, some cooks make an easier, but equally satisfying, baked pie version.

FOR THE CRUST

2 tablespoons extra-virgin olive oil, plus more for greasing

1 medium yellow onion, coarsely chopped

2 cups fine- or medium-grain bulgur, prepared according to package directions

¼ cup all-purpose flour

2 teaspoons kosher salt

½ teaspoon ground allspice

Freshly ground black pepper

FOR THE FILLING

Extra-virgin olive oil

1 large onion, finely chopped

1 pound ground beef or turkey

1 teaspoon ground cinnamon

1 teaspoon ground allspice

Kosher salt

Freshly ground black pepper

½ cup pine nuts

Cayenne pepper (optional)

TO MAKE THE CRUST

1. Preheat the oven to 375°F. Grease a 9-inch pie dish with olive oil.

2. In a food processor, process the onion until nearly pureed. Add the bulgur, olive oil, flour, salt, allspice, and pepper. Process until a loose paste forms.

TO MAKE THE FILLING

3. In a large nonstick skillet over medium-high heat, warm a thin layer of olive oil. Add the onion and cook, stirring frequently, about 3 minutes or until softened. Add the beef, cinnamon, allspice, and salt and pepper to taste. Cook until browned, 3 to 6 minutes. Stir in the pine nuts.

TO MAKE THE PIE

4. Press about half the dough into the bottom and sides of the pie dish. Add the filling. Press the remaining dough together on top of the filling to cover completely. Cut the uncooked pie into wedges, and brush the top with oil and sprinkle with red pepper, if using.

5. Bake the pie until golden brown and slightly crisped, about 45 minutes. Cool 15 minutes; serve warm or at room temperature.

Israeli Couscous with Tomato and Onion

KOSHER, VEGETARIAN / SERVES 4 TO 6
PREP TIME: 10 minutes, plus 30 minutes resting time / **COOK TIME:** 10 minutes

Israeli couscous, or ptitim, was created just after independence in the 1950s to meet the need for an inexpensive starch during a period of austerity. This tiny but versatile pearl-shaped, pasta-like staple remains popular, featured in everything from salads to stews. In this recipe, I've paired the slightly nutty couscous with a tomato-and-onion combination, typical of Middle Eastern cuisine.

---

1 (8-ounce) package Israeli couscous, cooked according to the package directions

3 tablespoons extra-virgin olive oil

3 tablespoons red wine vinegar

Kosher salt

Freshly ground black pepper

1 pound ripe tomatoes, cut into ½-inch dice

½ medium red onion, finely chopped, or 6 scallions, finely chopped with some large green pieces for color

½ cup fresh basil or mint leaves, chopped, plus a few whole leaves for garnish

Chopped fresh chives, for alternate garnish (optional)

---

1. In a large bowl, toss the still-warm couscous with the olive oil, vinegar, and salt and pepper to taste. Let cool slightly.

2. Stir in the tomatoes, onion, and basil leaves. Let stand at room temperature for 30 minutes to allow the flavors to meld.

3. Season to taste and serve at room temperature or chilled, garnished with whole herb leaves or chopped chives, if using.

INGREDIENT TIP: Be sure to use Israeli couscous, which has larger granules and a nuttier flavor than regular couscous.

Romanian-Style Polenta (Mamaliga)

GLUTEN-FREE, KOSHER, VEGETARIAN / SERVES 4
PREP TIME: 5 minutes / **COOK TIME:** 20 minutes

When corn and cornmeal were introduced to Eastern Europe, Romanians—including Romanian Jews—made use of it in porridge. Served soft or in slices, "mamaliga" (Romanian for "food of gold") was enjoyed at breakfast, lunch, dinner, and as a side or a snack. Creamy and comforting, it's served plain or with sour cream, jam, raw sliced onions, sautéed mushrooms, or with cheese on top or mixed in, as in this recipe.

---

1 cup milk

2 cups water

¼ teaspoon kosher salt, plus more
 to taste

1 cup medium-grind yellow cornmeal

3 tablespoons butter

¾ cup grated Parmesan

Freshly ground black pepper

---

1. In a medium saucepan over medium-high heat, combine the milk and water. Bring to a boil and add salt. Reduce the heat to a simmer and add in cornmeal in a slow, steady stream, whisking constantly to incorporate.

2. Return the heat to medium-high and bring the mixture to a boil, then reduce to low so mixture reaches a gentle simmer. Cook for about 20 minutes, stirring thoroughly every few minutes.

3. Remove from the heat, stir in the butter and cheese, and add salt and pepper to taste. Serve immediately.

VARIATION TIP: For firmer texture, spread the polenta in a lightly buttered pie dish and cool for 20 minutes. Slice into wedges and serve.

Persian-Style Jeweled Rice

GLUTEN-FREE, KOSHER, VEGETARIAN / SERVES 6 TO 8
PREP TIME: 20 minutes / **COOK TIME:** 55 minutes, plus resting time

Rice is a crown jewel of Iranian and Iranian-Jewish cooking. Very popular are saffron-scented rice dishes with delectable crispy-bottomed crusts, called tahdig. Perhaps even more prized are jeweled rice recipes like this one that add colorful fruits and fragrant spices to create a beautiful and special dish.

½ teaspoon saffron threads, crushed

¼ cup boiling water

2 cups basmati rice, well rinsed and drained

Kosher salt

½ cup chopped dried apricots

½ cup currants or raisins

½ cup dried barberries, dried cranberries, or dried sour cherries

5 tablespoons extra-virgin olive oil, divided

1 large sweet onion, finely chopped

Freshly ground black pepper

1 teaspoon ground cinnamon

1 teaspoon ground allspice

½ cup chopped salted pistachios, lightly toasted

¼ cup pomegranate seeds (optional)

1. Soak saffron in the boiling water for 10 minutes. Set aside.

2. In a large saucepan over medium heat, bring 1 quart of salted water to a boil. Add rice, cover, and cook for 6 to 8 minutes until al dente, stirring occasionally. Drain well and set aside. (It will finish cooking later.)

3. In a medium bowl, combine the dried apricots, currants, and barberries. Set aside.

4. Heat 1 tablespoon of olive oil in a large heavy pan such as a Dutch oven (preferably nonstick) over medium heat. Add the onion and season with salt and pepper to taste. Cook 3 to 5 minutes or until softened, stirring occasionally. Stir in the cinnamon and allspice. Transfer the mixture to a bowl and set aside. Wipe out the pan.

5. Return the pan to medium heat and add the remaining 4 tablespoons of oil. When hot, spread half the rice on the bottom and layer on the onions and the fruit mixture. Top with the remaining rice, pat down, and season lightly with salt and pepper. Cook uncovered for 10 to 14 minutes, until the rice down the sides and on the bottom just starts to brown. (It's okay to quickly peek.)

6. Drizzle the saffron mixture over the top and cover tightly. Reduce heat to lowest setting and cook 30 minutes, then turn off heat and let rest 10 minutes.

7. Spoon loose rice onto a platter, stirring to distribute the fruits. Using a spatula, carefully lift the remaining crusty rice out of the pan in large pieces. Place them browned-side up on the platter. Sprinkle with pistachios and pomegranate seeds, if using, and serve.

INGREDIENT TIP: Find the traditional tangy barberries in specialty stores or online.

Mujaddara (Middle Eastern Rice and Lentils)

GLUTEN-FREE, KOSHER, VEGETARIAN / SERVES 4 TO 6 (MAKES 6 TO 7 CUPS)
PREP TIME: 10 minutes / **COOK TIME:** 30 minutes

Variations of rice and lentils with onions have been comfort food for centuries across the Middle East. This relatively easy and filling vegetarian dish with caramelized onions was sometimes cooked and served on Thursday nights, before families began Shabbat preparations. Some recipes call for allspice or other warm spices—in this recipe, it's your choice.

1 cup green lentils

3 cups water

Kosher salt

¼ cup extra-virgin olive oil

1 cup basmati rice, well rinsed and drained

3 large red onions, halved and thinly sliced

Freshly ground black pepper

½ teaspoon ground allspice, cumin, or cinnamon (optional)

1. In a large saucepan over medium heat, combine the lentils with 3 cups of salted water. Bring to a boil, and then cover and simmer for 20 minutes.

2. Meanwhile, warm the olive oil in a large nonstick skillet over medium-high heat. Add the onions, season with salt and pepper to taste, and stir to combine. Turn the heat to low, cover, and cook undisturbed for 15 minutes, until the onions are soft and starting to brown. Remove a third of the onions, coarsely chop them, and set aside.

3. Turn the heat to high, and continue caramelizing the remaining onions in the pan for 3 to 5 minutes or until dark and slightly crispy, stirring frequently. Remove them from the pan and set aside.

4. Once the lentils have cooked for 20 minutes, stir in the rice, chopped onions, and allspice, if using. Cover and simmer 12 to 15 minutes, until the grains are tender. Drain any excess water and season to taste. Transfer to a serving bowl and toss with reserved caramelized onions. Serve warm.

Swiss Chard with Chickpeas

GLUTEN-FREE, KOSHER, VEGETARIAN / SERVES 4
PREP TIME: 20 minutes / **COOK TIME:** 30 minutes

Swiss chard with chickpeas is a favored combination with origins in Spain that appears in Sephardi cooking in Greece and Morocco. The chickpeas in this dish make it a substantial, filling side or a vegetarian main—and a nutritious one at that.

Extra-virgin olive oil

1 large sweet onion, finely chopped

Kosher salt

Freshly ground black pepper

3 garlic cloves, slivered

⅛ teaspoon crushed red pepper flakes

2 large bunches red Swiss chard, stems and ribs discarded, leaves coarsely chopped

1 cup seeded and diced plum tomatoes

1 (15.5-ounce) can chickpeas, rinsed and drained

1 cup low-sodium vegetable broth

Juice of ½ small lemon

1. In a large nonstick skillet over medium-high heat, warm a layer of oil. Add the onion, season lightly with salt and pepper to taste, and cook, stirring frequently, 3 to 5 minutes or until softened.

2. Add the garlic and red pepper flakes, and cook for 1 minute, stirring constantly. Add half the chard to the pan and fold until it wilts, then stir in the remaining chard. Add the tomatoes, chickpeas, broth, and additional salt to taste.

3. Reduce the heat to medium and cover. Cook, stirring occasionally, until the greens are just tender, 15 to 20 minutes. Remove the lid, increase the heat to medium-high, and boil until the remaining liquid is mostly evaporated, about 10 minutes.

4. To serve, transfer to a platter and squeeze lemon juice over the top.

Black-Eyed Peas with Tomatoes

GLUTEN-FREE, KOSHER, VEGETARIAN / SERVES 4 TO 6
PREP TIME: 10 minutes / **COOK TIME:** 35 minutes

Black-eyed peas are a common New Year's tradition in the American South, but they also have much older roots as a Rosh Hashanah food. Black-eyed peas are popular in Jewish communities in North Africa, Turkey, and the Balkans. As symbols of abundance and prosperity, these beans became featured in a Jewish new year's dish called lubiya. Serve this spicy and satisfying Egyptian- and Turkish-inspired version as an appetizer or main dish with rice or bread.

Extra-virgin olive oil

1 large onion, chopped

Kosher salt

Freshly ground black pepper

3 garlic cloves, minced

½ teaspoon ground allspice

¼ teaspoon crushed red pepper flakes

2 (15.5-ounce) cans black-eyed peas, drained

1 (14-ounce) can diced tomatoes with juices

1 tablespoon tomato paste

1 cup water

1. Warm a thin layer of oil in a 3-quart saucepan or stock pot over medium-high heat. Add the onion and season with salt and pepper to taste. Cook until softened, 3 to 5 minutes, stirring frequently.

2. Add the garlic, allspice, and red pepper flakes and cook, stirring constantly for 1 minute. Stir in the black-eyed peas, tomatoes, tomato paste, and water.

3. Cover, reduce heat to low, and simmer for 30 minutes. Season to taste and serve hot.

VARIATION TIP: For a smoky accent, use fire-roasted diced tomatoes.

Egyptian-Style Fava Beans

GLUTEN-FREE, KOSHER, VEGETARIAN / SERVES 2 TO 4
PREP TIME: 10 minutes / **COOK TIME:** 25 minutes

*Fava beans are popular in Middle Eastern cooking but especially
in Egypt, where slow-cooked ful medames is a staple. Egypt's Jews
adopted the dish as an overnight Sabbath stew. Serve this quicker
modern version with bread and yogurt or Garlic and Za'atar Labneh
(page 64). For a traditional take, lightly mash the beans before serving.*

1½ tablespoons extra-virgin olive
  oil, divided
1 medium red onion, finely chopped
½ teaspoon kosher salt, plus more
  to taste
Freshly ground black pepper
2 garlic cloves, minced

2 teaspoons cumin
¼ teaspoon cayenne pepper
2 (14-ounce) cans fava beans, drained
½ cup vegetable broth or water
2 teaspoons freshly squeezed lemon juice
2 tablespoons chopped cilantro (optional)

---

1. Warm 1 tablespoon of olive oil in a medium saucepan over medium-high heat. Add the onion, season with salt and pepper, and cook, stirring frequently until softened, 3 to 5 minutes.

2. Add the garlic, cumin, and cayenne pepper and cook for 1 minute, stirring constantly.

3. Stir in the beans, the remaining ½ teaspoon salt, pepper to taste, and ½ cup of broth or water. Bring the beans to a boil, then cover and reduce the heat to simmer until slightly thickened, about 20 minutes.

4. Remove from the heat. Stir in the lemon juice and remaining ½ tablespoon of olive oil. Season to taste, garnish with cilantro (if using), and serve hot.

VARIATION TIP: For a heartier dish (or for breakfast), top with hard-boiled, poached, or scrambled eggs.

Challah
Page 140

Chapter 8

Breads

BRAIDED BREAD

Challah: braided and golden, it's the revered centerpiece of the Shabbat table. Although the general concept of breads for Shabbat goes back to ancient times, challah is a relatively new creation. For centuries, Sabbath breads were flat-breads. "Challah" was a term referring to thickness, and later, a portion of dough broken off as a symbolic offering.

It wasn't until the fifteenth century that German and Austrian Jews, influenced by their neighbors' braided breads, began braiding loaves for Shabbat. Ashkenazi Jews brought braided challah to Eastern Europe and eventually to the United States. Only in twentieth-century America did braided, enriched bread become widely known as challah. And yet, it still didn't have a lock on Shabbat.

An entirely separate strand of breadmaking existed among Sephardi and Mizrahi Jews, who developed other customs for their Shabbat breads (such as naan among India's Jews or pita-like loaves among Yemenite Jews). They flavored their flatbreads with spices, dried fruits, seeds, nuts, olive oil, and saffron.

Today, challah refers to almost any Shabbat or special-occasion bread, and it takes on symbolic shapes, like when braided round on Rosh Hashanah to represent the cyclical nature of life. Nonetheless, challah—braided or otherwise—stands as a weekly connection to age-old Jewish tradition.

Express Bagels

FAMILY-FRIENDLY, KOSHER, VEGETARIAN / MAKES 6 BAGELS
PREP TIME: 10 minutes / **COOK TIME:** 20 minutes

From humble beginnings in Poland and the Baltics, the bagel became an everyday staple that Eastern European Jews later brought to New York. With a modern shortcut (borrowed from a viral recipe), you can make hot fresh bagels at home in no time. These express bagels are lighter-flavored and doughier than bakery bagels, but they're still wonderful. Lightly press on your favorite toppings before baking.

2¼ cups self-rising flour, plus more
   as needed
½ teaspoon kosher salt

2 (5.3-ounce) containers plain nonfat
   Greek yogurt (do not substitute regu-
   lar yogurt)
Olive oil or cooking spray

---

1. Preheat the oven to 375°F and line a sheet pan with parchment paper.

2. In a large bowl, combine the flour, salt, and yogurt, adding additional flour if needed to form a dough. Knead a few minutes until smooth.

3. Divide the dough into 6 pieces. Roll these into 8-inch long ropes and seal the ends together to make rings.

4. Place the rings on the sheet pan and lightly spray the tops with olive oil. Bake until golden, about 20 minutes. Serve warm.

Challah

FAMILY-FRIENDLY, KOSHER, VEGETARIAN / MAKES 1 LARGE LOAF
PREP TIME: 40 minutes, plus rising time / **COOK TIME:** 30 minutes

Challah is a staple of Shabbat for Jews around the world, and it also might be the most delicious and beautiful bread you'll ever pull out of your oven. Because challah doughs use eggs and sugar, they're sweeter and fluffier than your average bread. Don't let the braiding intimidate you—even a simple twist works just fine.

2¼ teaspoons (1 packet) active dry yeast

¾ cup warm water

¼ cup honey

2 teaspoons kosher salt, plus more for egg wash

2 eggs

⅓ cup olive or other vegetable oil, plus more for the bowl

3½ to 4 cups bread flour

Sesame or poppy seeds, optional

Egg wash (1 egg lightly beaten with 1 teaspoon water and pinch of salt)

---

1. In a large bowl, dissolve the yeast in the warm water for about 5 minutes. Stir in the honey, salt, eggs, and olive oil. Add 3 cups of the flour and stir to incorporate. Gradually add ½ cup more, and then more in small increments until the dough forms a soft, sticky mass.

2. Knead the dough until smooth and elastic, 12 to 14 minutes. Transfer the dough to an oiled bowl, turn over, and cover.

3. Let the dough rise in a warm place until doubled in size, 1½ to 2 hours. Once risen, punch down the dough, cover, and let it rest 15 minutes.

4. Transfer the dough to a lightly floured surface. Cut it into 3 pieces, roll those into 12-inch ropes, and braid, tucking under both ends. (Once you get comfortable with it, alternate braiding methods include 4- and 6-strand braids.)

5. Transfer the braided bread to a sheet pan lined with parchment paper. Brush the loaf with egg wash and top with seeds, if using.

6. Cover the dough with oiled plastic wrap and let rise 30 to 45 minutes, until a finger pressed into the dough leaves an imprint.

7. Meanwhile, preheat the oven to 350°F.

8. Bake the challah for 25 to 35 minutes, until it is golden brown and hollow-sounding when tapped. (An instant-read thermometer should read 190° to 195°F when inserted at the thickest point.) Let cool on a wire rack for at least 15 minutes before serving.

> **MAKE AHEAD TIP:** Make the dough a day ahead and let it rise overnight in the refrigerator. Set it out at room temperature 30 minutes before continuing with the recipe.

Sweet Challah

FAMILY-FRIENDLY, KOSHER, VEGETARIAN / MAKES 1 LARGE LOAF
PREP TIME: 40 minutes, plus rising time / **COOK TIME:** 35 minutes

Sweet challahs are particularly symbolic for Rosh Hashanah, representing the hope for a sweet new year. These holiday loaves are often braided or twisted into a round, symbolizing the cyclical nature of life.

2¼ teaspoons (1 packet) active dry yeast

¾ cup warm water

⅓ cup vegetable oil, plus more for coating the bowl

⅓ cup honey

2 teaspoons kosher salt

2 teaspoons vanilla extract

2 eggs, lightly beaten

4 to 4½ cups bread flour

1½ teaspoons cinnamon

½ cup dark raisins

Egg wash (1 egg lightly beaten with 1 teaspoon water and pinch of salt)

Coarse sugar for topping, optional

---

1. In a large bowl, dissolve the yeast in the warm water (about 5 minutes). Stir in the oil, honey, salt, vanilla extract, and eggs. Mix in 4 cups of the flour and the cinnamon. Stir in additional flour in small increments to form a soft, sticky dough.

2. Knead until the dough is smooth and elastic, 10 to 12 minutes, then knead in the raisins.

3. Transfer the dough to an oiled bowl, turn over, and cover. Let it rise in a warm place until doubled, 1 to 2 hours.

4. Deflate the dough, cover, and let rest 5 minutes.

5. Shape the dough into a 24-inch rope, tapered on one end. Twist the narrow end in a circle around the wide end, making a large pinwheel. Tuck the loose end underneath.

6. Transfer to a sheet pan lined with parchment paper. Brush with egg wash and top with coarse sugar, if using. Cover in oiled plastic wrap and let rise 30 to 45 minutes, until a finger pressed into the dough leaves an imprint.

7. Meanwhile, adjust the rack to the lower third of the oven and preheat to 350°F.

8. Bake for 30 to 40 minutes, until the loaf is golden brown and hollow-sounding when tapped. (An instant-read thermometer should read 190° to 195°F when inserted at the thickest point.) Let cool on a wire rack for at least 15 minutes before serving.

INGREDIENT TIP: To keep it fresh, store active dry yeast in the refrigerator or freezer.

Nutella Babka

FAMILY-FRIENDLY, KOSHER, VEGETARIAN / MAKES 2 LOAVES
PREP TIME: 40 minutes, plus rising time / **COOK TIME:** 25 minutes

From Poland and Ukraine, babka is a sweet yeasted cake whose name comes from the Slavic "babcia," meaning grandmother. In America, this decadent treat catapulted from Jewish bakeries to nationwide fame, spurred partially by an episode of Seinfeld. *Nutella provides an easy and sublimely rich filling. (It's somewhat messy but entirely worth it.)*

2¼ teaspoons (1 packet) active dry yeast

½ cup warm water

¼ cup sugar

½ teaspoon kosher salt

1 egg, plus 2 egg yolks

1 teaspoon vanilla extract

8 tablespoons (1 stick) butter, softened, plus more for greasing

3½ cups all-purpose flour, plus more as needed

1 cup Nutella

---

1. In a large bowl, dissolve the yeast in the warm water (about 5 minutes). Stir in the sugar, salt, egg, egg yolks, vanilla extract, and butter and then stir in the flour, adding more as needed to form a soft dough.

2. Knead the dough until smooth, about 4 minutes. Transfer to an oiled bowl, turn over, and cover. Let it rise in a warm place until doubled in size, about 1 hour.

3. Meanwhile, grease two 9-by-4-inch loaf pans.

4. Once risen, deflate the dough and divide it in half.

5. Take one half and roll to a roughly 12-by-13-inch rectangle on a lightly floured surface. Spread with half the Nutella, leaving a 1-inch border.

6. Starting with the shorter edge, roll into a log and seal the seam and ends. With a sharp knife, slice the log vertically in half and rest the halves side by side. (It will look messy.)

7. Gently twist these two halves together, filling-side up, by crossing one half over the other two or three times.

8. Transfer to one of the pans, filling-side up, squishing to fit.

9. Repeat steps 5 through 8 with the remaining dough.

10. Cover the loaves and let rise in a warm place until double in volume, 20 to 45 minutes.

11. Meanwhile, preheat the oven to 350°F.

12. Bake the loaves for 18 to 25 minutes, until lightly browned. Let cool in the pans for 10 minutes, then transfer to a wire rack to finish cooling. Serve warm or at room temperature.

Rye Bread

KOSHER, VEGETARIAN / MAKES 1 LOAF
PREP TIME: 25 minutes, plus rising and resting time / **COOK TIME:** 45 minutes

After challah, rye bread is perhaps the second best-known Jewish bread in America, and no wonder—it's a perfect complement to pastrami and corned beef sandwiches at Jewish delis. This recipe creates a crusty, dense, deeply flavored bread. Make the dough the night before baking.

2¼ teaspoons (1 packet) active dry yeast

¾ cup warm water, plus more as needed

2 tablespoons olive oil

1 tablespoon honey

½ tablespoon kosher salt

1½ cups bread flour, plus more as needed

1½ cups rye flour

2 tablespoons caraway seeds, plus more for topping

Olive oil cooking spray

---

1. In a large bowl, dissolve the yeast in the warm water (about 5 minutes). Stir in 1 more tablespoon of water, oil, honey, salt, bread flour, rye flour, and caraway seeds.

2. Knead until smooth and elastic, about 12 minutes, adding water or flour as needed to make it workable.

3. Transfer the dough to an oiled bowl, turn over, and cover. Let it rise overnight in the refrigerator.

4. Deflate the dough, cover, and let rest for 30 minutes at room temperature.

5. Meanwhile, line a sheet pan with parchment paper.

6. Shape the dough into an 8- to 10-inch-long oval loaf. Place it on the sheet pan, cover, and let rise in a warm place until nearly doubled in size, 1 to 2 hours.

7. Meanwhile, preheat the oven to 375°F.

8. Coat the dough with cooking spray and sprinkle with caraway seeds. Make 5 ¼-inch-deep diagonal cuts on top.

9. Bake for 30 to 40 minutes, until browned. (An instant-read thermometer inserted in the center should give a reading between 205° and 210°F.) Cool on a wire rack.

Spicy Cheese Biscuits (Boyikos)

KOSHER, VEGETARIAN / MAKES 10 TO 12 BISCUITS
PREP TIME: 15 minutes / **COOK TIME:** 20 minutes

Boyikos and their larger version, boyos, are Sephardi cheese pastries of various shapes and forms. Here an easy biscuit-style version creates finely flaky biscuits with a spicy finish. This recipe is adapted from recipes by chef and food historian Joyce Goldstein. Olive oil is traditional, but melted, slightly cooled butter can be substituted.

2½ cups all-purpose flour

2 teaspoons baking powder

1 teaspoon kosher salt

½ teaspoon red pepper flakes, minced

Freshly ground black pepper

1 cup shredded sharp cheddar cheese, plus more for topping

¾ cup olive oil

¼ cup cold water

1. Preheat the oven to 350°F and line a sheet pan with parchment paper.

2. In a large bowl, combine the flour, baking powder, salt, red pepper flakes, and black pepper to taste. Stir in the cheese, then the oil and water to form a dough.

3. Transfer the dough to a flat surface and press until about ½ inch thick. Cut rounds with a 2½-inch biscuit cutter.

4. Place the biscuits on the prepared sheet pan and sprinkle with the remaining cheese. Bake until lightly browned, about 20 minutes. Serve warm or at room temperature.

Pita Bread

FAMILY-FRIENDLY, KOSHER, VEGETARIAN / MAKES 6 FLATBREADS
PREP TIME: 20 minutes, plus rising time / **COOK TIME:** 10 minutes

Flatbreads have been predominant in the Middle East since pre-historic times. Out of this tradition evolved pita, a round loaf with a natural pocket. Today it is a favorite in Israel, where it serves as a fast-food sandwich bread as well as utensil for scooping up dips and sauces. Homemade is far superior to store-bought, and it's easier than you might think. Serve with Israeli-Style Chopped Salad (page 42) and Falafel (page 88).

1½ teaspoons active dry yeast

1 cup warm water

2½ teaspoons kosher salt

1 tablespoon extra-virgin olive oil, plus more for the bowl

3 cups bread flour, plus more as needed

1. In a large bowl, dissolve the yeast in the warm water, about 5 minutes. Stir in the salt, oil, and flour to form a slightly sticky dough, adding more flour as needed. Knead for 5 to 7 minutes, until smooth and elastic.

2. Transfer the dough to an oiled bowl, turn over, and cover. Place in a warm spot and let rise until doubled in size, 1½ to 2 hours.

3. Place a sheet pan or baking stone in the oven. Preheat to 500°F.

4. Deflate the dough and let rest for 5 minutes, then divide it into 6 balls. On a lightly floured surface, press each ball into a disk. Roll into smooth 6- to 7-inch circles, avoiding creases. Keep covered until they go in the oven.

5. Transfer the rounds directly to the sheet pan in the oven, working in batches. Bake until puffy and the bottoms just begin to brown, 2 to 8 minutes. Cool on a wire rack, then serve.

Khachapuri

KOSHER, VEGETARIAN / SERVES 4 / PREP TIME: 25 minutes / **COOK TIME:** 20 minutes

In Georgia (the country), traditional fare includes many versions of bread stuffed with melted cheese. This open-faced, boat-shaped version topped with an egg, called adjaruli khachapuri, became popular among Georgian Jews and later in Israel, where it is still widely enjoyed today. In this version feta and oregano make a flavorful filling (good even without the egg).

1 package store-bought pizza dough
1½ cups shredded mozzarella cheese
1½ cups crumbled feta
1 teaspoon dried oregano
Kosher salt

Freshly ground black pepper
All-purpose flour, for dusting
4 small or medium eggs
Extra-virgin olive oil

1. Preheat the oven to 450°F and line a sheet pan with parchment paper.

2. In a medium bowl, combine the mozzarella, feta, oregano, and salt and pepper to taste. Set aside.

3. Divide the dough into 4 balls. On a lightly floured surface, stretch and roll the dough balls into ovals, about ¼ inch thick, 5½ inches wide, and 8½ inches long.

4. Place ¼ of the filling in the center of each oval. Roll up the edges to create a football shape surrounding the filling, making sure there's enough of a border to hold in the egg later. Twist and seal the narrow ends.

5. Transfer to the prepared sheet pan and brush the crusts with oil. Bake until lightly browned, 10 to 15 minutes.

6. Remove the boats from the oven and crack an egg into each one. Return to the oven for 3 to 5 more minutes, until the eggs are cooked to your preference. Serve warm.

✳ Blintz Pancakes

KOSHER, VEGETARIAN / MAKES 10 TO 12 PANCAKES
PREP TIME: 10 minutes, plus chilling time/ **COOK TIME:** 15 minutes

All blintzes begin with a thin pancake, usually a thicker, slightly springier cousin of crepes. Use this recipe for Cheese Blintzes with Blueberry Sauce (page 18) or your preferred filling.

2 cups whole milk	4 eggs
2 tablespoons unsalted butter, melted and cooled slightly, plus 2 tablespoons more for the pan	1½ cups all-purpose flour
	½ teaspoon kosher salt

1. Combine the milk, butter, eggs, flour, and salt in a blender. Blend on low speed until smooth; refrigerate for 30 minutes.

2. Warm a 10-inch nonstick skillet over medium heat. Brush with a thin coat of melted butter. Once the skillet is hot, stream in ¼ cup of batter to evenly coat the bottom. Cook until the top is set, edges are dry, and bottom is lightly golden, about 60 seconds.

3. Loosen the cooked pancake and turn it out flat onto a plate, browned-side up. Repeat with remaining batter, stacking the pancakes as you go.

STORAGE TIP: The pancakes can be covered and refrigerated for up to 2 days.

Matzah

VEGETARIAN / MAKES 6 LARGE CRACKERS
PREP TIME: 10 minutes / **COOK TIME:** 12 minutes

Even though it's nearly impossible to create kosher-for-Passover matzah at home, this easy recipe is still a worthwhile endeavor that shows how good matzah can taste fresh out of the oven.

---

2 cups all-purpose flour
1 teaspoon kosher salt, plus more
   for topping

½ cup plus 1 tablespoon water
1 tablespoon extra-virgin olive oil

---

1. Preheat the oven to 500°F. Line 2 large sheet pans with parchment paper.

2. In a large bowl, mix the flour and salt. Add the water and the oil. Knead for a few minutes to form a dough.

3. Divide the dough into 6 parts. On a smooth surface, flatten and roll each as thinly as possible into rough circles or ovals.

4. Transfer to the sheet pans and use a fork to poke holes all over. Bake, turning once, until browned, 8 to 12 minutes.

KOSHER TIP: Although kosher for everyday use, this recipe is not kosher for Passover.

Cheesecake
Page 168

Chapter 9

Desserts

FOR THE LOVE OF CHOCOLATE

The next time you enjoy chocolate cake, remember that back in the seventeenth century, Jewish bakers in Italy and France were among the first to add chocolate and vanilla to cakes. Later, Hungarian Jews added chocolate filling to cake rolls, and Polish bakers laced it through babka. In Austria, Jewish baker Franz Sacher used chocolate to invent the famed Sacher torte (chocolate cake and apricot jam).

But how did chocolate arrive in Europe, and why were Jews pioneers in using it? The story begins on the Iberian Peninsula. When explorers returned to Spain from the Americas, they brought back cacao beans and a cacao drink recipe that when mixed with sugar, vanilla, and cinnamon charmed the Spanish aristocracy. Jews fleeing Spain and Portugal after 1492 carried knowledge of chocolate making (and its deliciousness) and their trading connections with them. They began importing cacao and making chocolate in places like Italy, Amsterdam, and Bayonne, France, where they established the country's first chocolate factories.

When Jews came to the United States so did their chocolate-making. One Austrian Jewish immigrant launched what became Barton's Candies, one of the first commercial enterprises to produce kosher-certified goods—even kosher chocolate Santas. The Jews weren't the first to love chocolate, but they played a key role in its evolution into the product we know and widely love today.

Mandelbrot

KOSHER, VEGETARIAN / MAKES ABOUT 24 COOKIES
PREP TIME: 30 minutes / **COOK TIME:** 1 hour

Mandelbrot are twice-baked sliced cookies beloved in Ashkenazi baking. They're similar to biscotti, but traditionally a bit more tender. Here, marzipan adds tenderness and a deeper almond flavor. This recipe even wins over people who don't think they like biscotti.

---

1 (7-ounce) package marzipan, shredded using the large holes of a box grater

1 cup sugar

½ cup (1 stick) unsalted butter, room temperature, or vegetable oil

1 cup almond flour

4 large eggs, lightly beaten

2 teaspoons vanilla extract

3 cups all-purpose flour

1 teaspoon baking powder

½ teaspoon baking soda

¼ teaspoon kosher salt

¾ cup slivered almonds

---

1. Preheat the oven to 350°F and line a large sheet pan with parchment paper.

2. In a large bowl, combine the marzipan and sugar to form a lumpy mixture. Work in the butter, and stir in the almond flour, eggs, and vanilla extract. Fold in the flour, baking powder, baking soda, salt, and almonds.

3. Form the dough into 2 loaves (about 2½ inches wide and 1 inch high) directly on the sheet pan. Bake for 30 to 40 minutes, until golden brown.

4. Slide the loaves still on the parchment onto a wire rack and cool for 10 minutes. Adjust the oven temperature to 325°F and line the pan with new parchment paper.

5. Use a long serrated knife to cut the loaves diagonally into ½- to ¾-inch-thick slices. Place slices flat on the sheet pan and bake 18 to 22 minutes or until toasted, flipping over halfway through. Cool on wire racks.

INGREDIENT TIP: For more almond flavor, substitute 1 teaspoon of almond extract for one of the teaspoons of vanilla extract.

Chocolate Rugelach

FAMILY-FRIENDLY, KOSHER, VEGETARIAN / MAKES 48 RUGELACH
PREP TIME: 30 minutes / **COOK TIME:** 30 minutes

An irresistible cross between a pastry and a cookie, rugelach have become one of the most popular Ashkenazic baked goods today, in many variations beyond the traditional cinnamon. Here a decadent dark chocolate filling takes center stage, deliciously. The cream cheese that makes the pastries flaky also makes the dough delicate. If it gets too sticky to roll, chill it for 5 to 10 minutes before proceeding.

FOR THE DOUGH

1 (8-ounce) package cream cheese, room temperature

1 cup (2 sticks) unsalted butter, room temperature

¼ cup sugar

⅛ teaspoon kosher salt

1½ teaspoons vanilla extract

2½ cups all-purpose flour, plus more as needed

FOR THE FILLING

8 ounces bittersweet chocolate, melted and cooled slightly

5 tablespoons butter, room temperature

2 tablespoons light brown sugar

2 tablespoons unsweetened cocoa powder

½ teaspoon ground cinnamon

FOR THE TOPPING

Egg wash (1 egg lightly beaten with 1 tablespoon milk and a pinch of salt)

Coarse sugar, for sprinkling (optional)

TO MAKE THE DOUGH

1. In a large bowl, cream the cheese and butter. Add the sugar, salt, and vanilla extract. Stir in the flour to make a sticky dough, adding more if needed.

2. Divide the dough into 4 balls. Between two sheets of wax paper, roll out each one to a 9- to 10-inch circle. Wrap and chill for 1 hour or overnight.

3. When ready to bake, preheat the oven to 350°F. Line 2 large sheet pans with parchment paper.

TO MAKE THE FILLING

4. In a medium bowl, combine the chocolate, butter, brown sugar, cocoa, and cinnamon to form a paste.

TO MAKE THE RUGELACH

5. Remove the dough from the refrigerator to soften for a few minutes before handling. Immediately spread each round with a quarter of the filling (a scant ⅓ cup), working quickly so the filling doesn't stiffen.

6. Cut each round into 12 triangular wedges. Starting at the wide edge, roll up each triangle jelly-roll style. Place the rugelach seam-side down on the pans and freeze 10 minutes.

7. Brush each rugelach with the egg wash and sprinkle with sugar, if using. Bake until lightly golden, 18 to 22 minutes. Cool on a wire rack.

Hamantaschen

FAMILY-FRIENDLY, KOSHER, VEGETARIAN / MAKES ABOUT 22 COOKIES
PREP TIME: 30 minutes, plus chilling time / **COOK TIME:** 20 minutes

These triangular filled pastries, eaten on Purim, get their name from the Purim story's vanquished villain Haman. Hamantaschen (Yiddish for "Haman's pockets") hold several symbolic meanings, but more than anything today, they are a relished Ashkenazi treat. Traditional filling choices include apricot, poppy seed, and prune, but you can use any preserves or spreads you like.

FOR THE DOUGH

½ cup (1 stick) unsalted butter, room
   temperature

⅔ cup sugar

2 eggs

2 tablespoons whole milk

1 teaspoon vanilla extract

¼ teaspoon kosher salt

1¼ teaspoons baking powder

2½ cups all-purpose flour, plus additional
   as needed

FOR TOPPING AND FILLING

Preserves (such as apricot or raspberry)
   or spread (such as Nutella) of choice

Egg wash (1 egg lightly beaten with
   1 tablespoon milk and a pinch of salt)

TO MAKE THE DOUGH

1. In a large bowl, cream the butter and sugar. Blend in the eggs, milk, and vanilla extract. Fold in the salt, baking powder, and flour, adding more flour if needed to form a soft dough.

2. Divide the dough into 2 balls. Between two sheets of wax paper, roll each ball to between ⅛- and ¼-inch thick. Wrap and chill at least 1 hour or overnight.

TO MAKE THE HAMANTASCHEN

3. When ready to bake, preheat the oven to 350°F and line two sheet pans with parchment paper.

4. Remove the dough from the refrigerator to soften 5 minutes before handling. Cut 3-inch rounds in the dough and fill each round with 1 heaping teaspoon of preserves. Fold up to form a triangle with a little filling showing in the center, pinching corners firmly to seal.

5. Transfer the triangles to the prepared sheet pans and freeze for 15 minutes.

6. Remove triangles from the freezer, re-pinch the corners, and brush with egg wash. Bake 19 to 20 minutes, until lightly browned. Cool on a wire rack.

VARIATION TIP: For a pretty and flavorful finish, drizzle cooled pastries with melted dark or white chocolate or a confectioners' sugar glaze (½ cup sugar, a pinch of salt, and water to make a pourable consistency).

Coconut Macaroons

GLUTEN-FREE, KOSHER, VEGETARIAN / MAKES ABOUT 20 COOKIES
PREP TIME: 15 minutes / **COOK TIME:** 15 minutes

Macaroons started as confections of ground almonds, sugar, and egg whites, probably spreading around the world through Muslim territory, Spain, and later Italy, where they got their modern name. Naturally flour-free, these cookies became a Passover favorite. In the United States coconut versions gained popularity, though far too many people have only tried them from a can. They're easy to make at home, and oh so good.

3 egg whites

½ cup sugar

½ cup almond flour

⅛ teaspoon kosher salt

1 teaspoon vanilla extract or flavoring

2½ cups shredded sweetened coconut

1. Preheat the oven to 350°F and line a sheet pan with parchment paper.

2. In a large bowl, beat the egg whites until stiff. Gently fold the sugar into the egg whites, then fold in the almond flour, salt, vanilla, and finally the coconut.

3. Drop tablespoonfuls of the mixture about an inch apart on the prepared pan. Bake for about 15 minutes, until just browning on the edges. Cool on a wire rack. Store for up to 3 days in an airtight container.

VARIATION TIP: For a pretty presentation, melt 2 ounces bittersweet chocolate to between 88° and 91°F and drizzle it over the baked macaroons. Let set before serving.

Apple Pie Egg Rolls

KOSHER, VEGETARIAN / MAKES 8 TO 10 EGG ROLLS
PREP TIME: 10 minutes / **COOK TIME:** 35 minutes

One of my family's Rosh Hashanah dessert traditions has always been apple pie or apple crostata. Fall's best apples melded with cinnamon and other spices create wonderful aromas in the kitchen, and it wouldn't be the holiday without them. For a fun twist, this recipe encloses that pie filling in egg roll wrappers to create individual pies quickly fried on your stovetop. They make a traditional yet quick and novel holiday or anytime treat.

¼ cup packed light brown sugar

2 teaspoons ground cinnamon

¼ teaspoon allspice (or nutmeg)

2 tablespoons all-purpose flour

2 large apples (Honeycrisp or Granny Smith), peeled, cored, and diced

Juice of 1 lemon

8 to 10 egg roll wrappers

Canola oil, for frying

¼ cup confectioners' sugar, for serving

---

1. In a medium mixing bowl, combine the brown sugar, cinnamon, allspice, and flour..

2. In a large bowl, combine the diced apples with the lemon juice. Add the brown sugar mixture and mix well.

3. Place 1 to 2 tablespoons of apples in the center of each egg roll wrapper, then wet the edges and roll up.

4. Line a plate with paper towels. Coat a large skillet with oil and place it over high heat. When the oil is hot, add the egg rolls and fry them until golden brown on all sides.

5. Place the fried egg rolls on the paper towel-lined plate to soak up excess oil, then dust them with confectioners' sugar.

Apple Cake

KOSHER, VEGETARIAN / SERVES 8 TO 10
PREP TIME: 20 minutes / **COOK TIME:** 55 minutes

Apples are featured prominently on Rosh Hashanah, symbolizing a sweet new year—and apple cakes are a standby Rosh Hashanah dessert in the Ashkenazi repertoire. The shredded apples in this Bundt version make for a moist cake that tastes even better the day after it's made.

---

1 cup mild olive oil or butter, melted and slightly cooled, plus more for greasing

4 cups all-purpose flour

1 teaspoon kosher salt

1½ teaspoons baking powder

½ teaspoon baking soda

1½ teaspoons ground cinnamon

1 teaspoon ground allspice

3 eggs

½ cup thawed frozen apple juice concentrate

1 cup light brown sugar

1 tablespoon vanilla extract

3 large apples, peeled and shredded (about 3 cups), such as Honeycrisp

---

1. Preheat the oven to 350°F. Grease a nonstick 12-cup Bundt pan.

2. In a medium bowl, whisk the flour, salt, baking powder, baking soda, cinnamon, and allspice to combine.

3. In a large bowl, whisk together the eggs, apple juice, oil, sugar, and vanilla extract. Stir in the dry ingredients and then fold in the shredded apples.

4. Transfer the batter to the Bundt pan and smooth the top. Bake until a tester inserted in the center comes out mostly clean, 35 to 45 minutes. If the cake appears to be browning too quickly, cover it loosely with a piece of foil after about 25 minutes.

5. Cool 10 minutes; then invert the cake on a wire rack and remove the pan. Cool before serving.

VARIATION TIP: Dust with confectioners' sugar or drizzle with a confectioners' sugar glaze.

Honey-Soaked Walnut Cake (Tishpishti)

KOSHER, VEGETARIAN / SERVES 8 TO 10
PREP TIME: 15 minutes / **COOK TIME:** 50 minutes, plus resting time

For Rosh Hashanah, honey cakes are a popular Ashkenazi dessert, but Sephardi and other Middle Eastern Jews bake syrup-soaked nut cakes in various styles, called tishpishti. This recipe, adapted from Joan Nathan's Jewish Cooking in America, creates a uniquely sweet, crumbly, and warmly spiced dessert.

½ cup olive oil, plus more for greasing

3 cups all-purpose flour

1 teaspoon baking powder

¼ teaspoon kosher salt

2 cups chopped walnuts

2 tablespoons light brown sugar

1 teaspoon ground cinnamon

¼ teaspoon ground cloves

Zest 1 medium orange

1 cup water, divided

1 teaspoon vanilla extract

1 cup honey

¼ cup sugar

¼ cup freshly squeezed orange juice

---

1. Preheat the oven to 350°F. Oil a 9-by-9-inch baking dish.

2. In a large bowl, combine the flour, baking powder, salt, walnuts, brown sugar, cinnamon, cloves, and orange zest. Gradually work in the oil, ½ cup of water, and vanilla extract, adding more water as needed to moisten the dough.

3. Press the dough evenly into the baking dish. Cut into squares or diamond shapes. Bake about 50 minutes, until dry and lightly browned.

4. Meanwhile, make the syrup. Combine the honey, sugar, orange juice, and ½ cup of water in a medium saucepan over low heat, stirring until the sugar dissolves. Gently boil for about 20 minutes and cool slightly.

5. Remove the cake from the oven and immediately pour the syrup over it. Let stand for at least 30 minutes before serving or cool, cover, and refrigerate for up to 2 days. Serve warm, room temperature, or slightly chilled.

Stuffed Figs

GLUTEN-FREE, KOSHER, VEGETARIAN / MAKES 20 STUFFED FIGS
PREP TIME: 10 minutes, plus chilling time / **COOK TIME:** 4 minutes

Native to the Mediterranean, figs have symbolic significance in the Hebrew Bible as one of seven special products of the Land of Israel. Among Sephardi and Mizrahi Jews, figs (and dates) are often eaten plain or stuffed with fillings like goat cheese, almond paste, or chocolate. My version, with a tangy, creamy cheese filling, makes a great appetizer or dessert.

4 ounces mild goat cheese, softened

4 ounces cream cheese, softened

½ teaspoon vanilla extract

¼ teaspoon kosher salt

20 large dried Turkish figs

Balsamic vinegar for drizzling, optional

1. In a medium bowl, combine the goat cheese, cream cheese, vanilla extract, and salt.

2. Cut the stems off the figs and gently open a cavity in the tops. Spoon the filling into the cavities.

3. Place the figs filling-side up on a small sheet pan and freeze for 15 minutes.

4. Meanwhile, preheat the broiler on high.

5. Broil figs 2 to 4 minutes, until the filling just begins to soften and bubble. Serve warm, drizzled with a couple of drops of balsamic vinegar, if using.

Flourless Chocolate Cake

GLUTEN-FREE, KOSHER, VEGETARIAN / SERVES 6 TO 8
PREP TIME: 30 minutes / **COOK TIME:** 35 minutes, plus chilling and resting time

This rich, intensely chocolatey flourless recipe takes the cake (literally)
among decadent yet gluten-free (and chametz-free) desserts.
Although always a big hit at Passover, this cake's dense, fudgy good-
ness elevates any occasion.

Cooking spray, for greasing the pan
Cocoa powder, for dusting the pan
12 ounces bittersweet chocolate,
   coarsely chopped
½ cup (1 stick) unsalted butter
1 tablespoon vanilla extract or flavoring

Pinch ground cinnamon
6 eggs, separated
⅓ cup sugar
Pinch kosher salt
Whipped cream, for serving

---

1. Adjust the rack to the lower third of the oven and preheat the oven to 325°F. Coat a 9-inch springform pan with cooking spray and dust it with cocoa powder.

2. In a small saucepan over low heat, melt the chocolate and butter. Remove it from the heat and stir in the vanilla extract or flavoring and cinnamon. Let cool slightly.

3. In a large bowl, whisk the egg yolks with the sugar and salt until slightly frothy and uniformly colored. Add to the chocolate mixture.

4. In a second large bowl, beat the egg whites on high speed until stiff peaks form, 1 to 2 minutes. In three additions, fold the egg whites into the chocolate mixture.

5. Transfer the batter to the springform pan and smooth the top. Place the pan on a sheet pan. Bake for 25 to 35 minutes, until brownie-like (and a cake tester comes out mostly clean). Cool 10 minutes on a wire rack, then unmold the cake.

6. Serve warm with whipped cream or chill overnight, letting rest at room temperature for 30 minutes before serving.

Cheesecake

FAMILY-FRIENDLY, KOSHER, VEGETARIAN / SERVES 6 TO 8
PREP TIME: 30 minutes / **COOK TIME:** 50 minutes, plus 6 hours cooling time

When cream cheese was invented in New York in 1872, Jewish bakers used it on more than just bagels. It made flakier pastry dough and became a substitute (with sour cream) for cottage cheese previously used in cheesecake. Thus, New York–style cheesecake was born. Cheesecake wows crowds year-round, but is especially welcomed for dairy-centric holidays like Hanukkah and Shavuot. This super-creamy version pairs beautifully with fruit.

FOR THE CRUST

4 tablespoons (½ stick) melted butter, divided

1½ cups crushed graham crackers (from about 10 full crackers)

1 tablespoon light brown sugar

⅛ teaspoon ground cinnamon

½ teaspoon vanilla extract

FOR THE FILLING

2 (8-ounce) packages cream cheese, room temperature

⅔ cup sugar

1 tablespoon cornstarch

3 eggs, room temperature

2 teaspoons vanilla extract

¼ teaspoon kosher salt

3 cups sour cream

1 to 2 pounds strawberries, sliced or quartered (optional)

TO MAKE THE CRUST

1. Adjust the rack to the lower third of the oven and preheat to 325°F. (Do not use convection bake setting.) Coat the sides and bottom of a 9-inch springform pan with ½ tablespoon of the melted butter. Line the bottom with parchment paper cut to size and brush with ½ tablespoon of butter.

2. In a medium bowl, combine the graham crackers, brown sugar, cinnamon, vanilla, and remaining 3½ tablespoons of butter. Press evenly into bottom of the springform pan.

TO MAKE THE FILLING

 3. In a large bowl with an electric mixer, beat the cream cheese and sugar on low speed just until smooth. Beat in the cornstarch. Add the eggs one at a time, beating at low speed, until just incorporated. Fold in the vanilla extract, salt, and sour cream.

 4. Pour the mixture into the crust and smooth the top. Tap the pan a few times on the counter to release any air bubbles. Place the pan on a sheet pan.

5. Bake 40 to 50 minutes, until the edges are set, but the center 3 inches still wiggle. (An instant-read thermometer should read 155°F when inserted in the center.)

6. Cool completely on a wire rack, then refrigerate, covered, at least 6 hours and up to 2 days. Remove the springform and serve chilled, garnished with strawberries (if using).

VARIATION TIP: For a slightly nutty flavor, add ¼ cup chopped pecans and an additional tablespoon of melted butter to the crust before pressing in the pan.

Sufganiyot (Jelly-Filled Donuts)

FAMILY-FRIENDLY, KOSHER, VEGETARIAN / MAKES ABOUT 40 SMALL DONUTS
PREP TIME: 45 minutes, plus chilling time overnight / **COOK TIME:** 10 minutes

In Israel, sufganiyot (jelly-filled donuts) are a near-ubiquitous fried food for Hanukkah, making their way via Jews from Germany. Named for the word for "spongy dough," sufganiyot have recently caught on in the United States. This recipe makes them bite-size and irresistible.

1¼ teaspoons active dry yeast

⅔ cups lukewarm milk

1 egg

4 tablespoons (½ stick) unsalted butter, melted and cooled slightly

2 tablespoons sugar, plus more for coating

½ teaspoon kosher salt

2¼ cups all-purpose flour, plus more as needed

Vegetable oil, for frying and oiling the bowl

Fruit jelly, about ¾ cup, for filling

---

1. In a large bowl, dissolve the yeast in the milk (about 5 minutes).

2. Whisk in the egg, butter, sugar, and salt. Stir in the flour, adding more as needed to form a soft, sticky dough. Knead the dough gently until smooth, 1 to 2 minutes. Transfer the dough to an oiled bowl, turn over, and cover. Refrigerate overnight.

3. The next day, deflate the dough and let rest, loosely covered, for 15 minutes at room temperature.

4. Roll pieces of dough into 1-inch balls. Place on a lightly floured sheet of parchment paper. Cover and let rise until puffy, about 45 minutes.

5. In a large heavy pan, heat 2 inches of oil to 360°F. Working in batches and reshaping as needed, fry the donuts until browned all over, 1 to 2 minutes. Transfer to a paper towel–lined plate.

6. Using a metal skewer, poke holes in the donuts and wiggle to create a cavity. Pipe or spoon in the jelly.

7. Roll the filled donuts in sugar and serve immediately.

Malabi

GLUTEN-FREE, KOSHER, VEGETARIAN / SERVES 6
PREP TIME: 10 minutes / **COOK TIME:** 12 minutes, plus cooling time

Malabi is a cool, creamy milk pudding popular throughout the Middle East. Different regions have their own traditional flavorings and toppings, but one of the most common is the lovely, fragrant pairing of rose water and nuts. Raspberry preserves add beautiful color and sweetness.

⅓ cup plus 1 tablespoon cornstarch

⅓ cup sugar

3½ cups whole milk, divided

1 teaspoon vanilla extract

1 cup raspberry preserves

½ cup water

1 teaspoon rose water (optional)

Chopped salted pistachios

1. In a large saucepan, combine the cornstarch and sugar. Stir in 3 to 4 tablespoons of the milk to make a slurry.

2. Gradually stir in the remaining milk and vanilla extract. Cook over medium-low heat stirring constantly, until mixture thickens, about 10 minutes.

3. Divide the pudding into 6 serving dishes. Cover with plastic wrap directly on the pudding's surface to prevent a skin from forming. Chill at least 4 hours.

4. To make the syrup: In a small saucepan over medium-high heat, bring the preserves and water to a gentle boil. Cook, stirring occasionally, for 10 minutes. Cool slightly, stir in the rose water (if using), and chill.

5. To serve, top the pudding with syrup and nuts.

Chapter 10

Menus

Shabbat and Jewish holidays create soothing and meaningful rhythms and rituals of Jewish life—and food plays an important role. Symbolic foods, special family dishes, and recipes celebrating the wide range of Jewish experience all serve up generous helpings of just what we need—nourishment, inspiration, comfort, and delight.

These menus, which combine foods from different Jewish traditions, offer a starting place for planning memorable meals and forming your own (delicious) traditions.

✴ Shabbat

Shabbat dinner on Friday nights is the most special of the week.

MEAT

Challah (page 140)

Classic Chicken Soup (page 66)

Lemon-Garlic Roast Chicken (page 97) or Chicken Sofrito (page 102)

Spinach with Raisins and Pine Nuts (page 50)

Mandelbrot (page 157) or Apple Cake (page 164)

VEGETARIAN/DAIRY

Challah (page 140)

Borscht (page 74)

Lentil "Pizzas" (page 80)

Stuffed Figs (page 166) or Blueberry and Cream Cheese Bourekas (page 23)

✴ Rosh Hashanah

New Year's dishes symbolically feature sweet, golden, or round foods.

Sweet Challah (page 142)

Black-Eyed Peas with Tomatoes (page 134)

Brisket with Red Wine and Tomatoes (page 104)

Maple, Carrot, and Sweet Potato Tzimmes (page 44)

Apple Cake (page 164) or Honey-Soaked Walnut Cake (page 165)

Yom Kippur Break-the-Fast

The stars for a break-the-fast are nourishing foods that can be made ahead or prepared quickly.

Moroccan Lentil Soup (page 65)

Huevos Haminados (page 28)

Malawach with Grated Tomato (page 30)

Smoked Whitefish Salad (page 29) with Express Bagels (page 139)

Pear and Mango Compote with Honey (page 25)

Malabi (page 171) or Sweet Cheese Noodle Kugel (page 121)

Sukkot

Dishes prepared for this harvest holiday often highlight fruits and vegetables and stuffed foods.

Roasted Butternut Squash Soup (page 75)

Roasted Vegetable Moussaka (page 82) or Turkey-Stuffed Cabbage (page 110)

Persian-Style Jeweled Rice (page 130)

Stuffed Figs (page 166) or Nutella Babka (page 144)

Hanukkah

Hanukkah features fried foods, symbolizing the oil that miraculously burned for eight nights.

Jewish-Italian Fried Chicken (page 98)

Classic Potato Latkes (page 37) with Cinnamon-Spiced Apple-sauce (page 61)

Swiss Chard with Chickpeas (page 133)

Sufganiyot (page 170) or Chocolate Rugelach (page 158)

Purim

This boisterous holiday features sweet and triangular foods and often vegetarian dishes (as well as some imbibing).

Kreplach (with cheese filling) (page 123) or Chickpea Sambousak (page 86)

Caponata (page 46)

Chocolate "Egg Cream" Ice Cream Soda (with bourbon) (page 32)

Hamantaschen (page 160)

Passover

The Seder (and accompanying dinner) is the main celebration of Passover, when eating leavened foods is prohibited.

MEAT

Apple and Walnut Haroset (page 39)

Wine-Poached Gefilte Fish (page 116) or North African–Style Spicy Fish (page 114)

Matzah Ball Soup (page 68)

Brisket with Red Wine and Tomatoes (page 104) or
Sephardi-Style Roast Lamb Shoulder (page 112)

Roasted Pepper Salad (page 51)

Coconut Macaroons (page 162)

DAIRY

Date and Apricot Haroset Balls (page 40)

Poached Salmon with Lemon-Dill Sauce (page 113)

Sephardi Spinach and Cheese Matzah Pie (page 91)

Tabbouleh (made with quinoa) (page 41)

Flourless Chocolate Cake (page 167)

✳ Shavuot

In accordance with ancient tradition, Shavuot often features dairy foods.

Garlic and Za'atar Labneh (page 64) with sliced vegetables

Spicy Cheese Biscuits (page 148)

Cheesy Stuffed Tomatoes (page 79)

Moroccan Orange and Black Olive Salad (page 48)

Cheese Blintzes with Blueberry Sauce (page 18) or Cheesecake
(page 168)

Measurement Conversions

VOLUME EQUIVALENTS (LIQUID)		
US Standard (ounces)	US Standard (approximate)	Metric
2 tablespoons	1 fl.oz.	30 mL
¼ cup	2 fl. oz.	60 mL
½ cup	4 fl. oz.	120 mL
1 cup	8 fl. oz.	240 mL
1½ cups	12 fl.oz.	355 mL
2 cups or 1 pint	16 fl. oz.	475 mL
4 cups or 1 quart	32 fl. oz.	1 L
1 gallon	128 fl.oz.	4 L

OVEN TEMPERATURES	
Fahrenheit (F)	Celsius (C) (approximate)
250°F	120°C
300°F	150°C
325°F	165°C
350°F	180°C
375°F	190°C
400°F	200°C
425°F	220°C
450°F	230°C

VOLUME EQUIVALENTS (DRY)	
US Standard	Metric (approximate)
⅛ teaspoon	0.5 mL
¼ teaspoon	1 mL
½ teaspoon	2 mL
¾ teaspoon	4 mL
1 teaspoon	5 mL
1 tablespoon	15 mL
¼ cup	60 mL
⅓ cup	79 mL
½ cup	120 mL
⅔ cup	156 mL
¾ cup	177 mL
1 cup	240 mL
2 cups or 1 pint	475 mL
3 cups	700 mL
4 cups or 1 quart	1 L

WEIGHT EQUIVALENTS	
US Standard	Metric (approximate)
½ ounce	15 g
1 ounce	30 g
2 ounces	60 g
4 ounces	115 g
8 ounces	225 g
12 ounces	340 g
16 ounces or 1 pound	455 g

Resources

There are many fascinating resources on Jewish food and food history. Here is a selection of those I found especially helpful.

Glezer, Maggie. *A Blessing of Bread: Recipes and Rituals, Memories and Mitzvahs.* New York: Artisan, 2004.

Goldman, Marcy. *A Treasury of Jewish Holiday Baking,* New York: Doubleday, 1998.

Goldstein, Joyce. *The New Mediterranean Jewish Table.* Oakland: University of California Press, 2016.

Goldstein, Joyce. *Sephardic Flavors: Jewish Cooking of the Mediterranean.* San Francisco: Chronicle Books, 2000.

Koenig, Leah. *The Jewish Cookbook.* London: Phaidon Press, 2019.

Marks, Copeland. *The Varied Kitchens of India: Cuisines of the Anglo-Indians of Calcutta, Bengalis, Jews of Calcutta, Kashmiris, Parsis, and Tibetans of Darjeeling.* Lanham, Md.: M. Evans, 1986.

Marks, Gil. *Encyclopedia of Jewish Food.* Hoboken, N.J.: John Wiley & Sons, 2010.

Marks, Gil. *Olive Trees and Honey: A Treasury of Vegetarian Recipes from Jewish Communities Around the World.* Boston: Houghton Mifflin Harcourt, 2005.

Nathan, Joan. *Jewish Cooking in America.* New York: Alfred A. Knopf, 1998.

Nathan, Joan. *King Solomon's Table.* New York: Alfred A. Knopf, 2017.

Newhouse, Alana. *The 100 Most Jewish Foods: A Highly Debatable List.* New York: Artisan, 2019.

Ottolenghi, Yotam and Sami Tamimi. *Jerusalem: A Cookbook.* Berkeley, Calif.: Ten Speed Press, 2012.

Prinz, Rabbi Deborah R. *On the Chocolate Trail: A Delicious Adventure Connecting Jews, Religions, History, Travel, Rituals and Recipes to the Magic of Cacao,* 2nd Edition. Nashville, Tenn.: Jewish Lights Publishing, 2018.

Roden, Claudia. *The Book of Jewish Food.* New York: Alfred A. Knopf, 2013.

Sarna, Shannon. *Modern Jewish Baker: Challah, Babka, Bagels, and More.* New York: The Countryman Press, 2017.

Index

Note: Page numbers in bold indicate photos.

Acknowledgments

I'm indebted to and grateful for the following people, who were instrumental in my creating this book:

The staff at Callisto Media, especially Elizabeth Castoria and Claire Yee, and also freelance developmental editor Allie Kiekofer.

Rabbi Avis Miller, who has long inspired me, for her initial feedback and encouragement.

My recipe testers and tasters—dear friends and family—who adopted these recipes into their kitchens and made them their own. The recipes are so much better for the patience and talents of Nikki DiNenna, Lisa LaCamera, Sandra Thompson, Amy Glancy, Victoria Rapoport, Bob Wilson, Josie Mani, and Chef Richard DiNenna.

My longtime friend and editor partner, Lisa Resnick, for her editorial expertise and always pointing my writing in the right direction.

My parents, Sandra and Berney, and my in-laws, Gloria and David, for their love and encouragement—lifelong gifts that keep on giving.

My husband Daryl, a true mensch, for his unwavering support, patient listening, brainstorming, emergency store runs, and being my everything, always—I love you.

ABOUT THE AUTHOR

Marcia Friedman is the author of *Meatballs and Matzah Balls: Recipes and Reflections from a Jewish and Italian Life* and serves on the Advisory Council of The Jewish Food Experience. She's been exploring and cooking Jewish and Italian foods for more than 20 years, developing and refining recipes for herself and home cooks everywhere. Her stories, quotes, and recipes have appeared in *Tablet*, the *Washington Post*, the *Jewish Food Experience*, the *Forward*, *Washington Jewish Week*, and *Interfaith Family*, among others. A writer, editor, photographer, and recipe developer, she particularly loves taking storied recipes and making them accessible and the best they can be. Visit her at meatballsandmatzahballs.com.

Printed in the USA
CPSIA information can be obtained
at www.ICGtesting.com
LVHW051929091223
765801LV00003B/21

9 781646 117277